ACHIEVING FLUENCY IN ENGLISH

A Whole-Language Book
3rd Edition

Adele MacGowan-Gilhooly
City College of the
City University of New York

KENDALL/HUNT PUBLISHING COMPANY
4050 Westmark Drive   Dubuque, Iowa 52002

This book is dedicated to
my husband, Edward J. Gilhooly,
with love.

What we learn with pleasure,
we never forget.

-Alfred Mercier

CONTENTS

PREFACE

The purpose of this book is to help students learn to write and to read fluently in English. It can be used over one semester or two. I wrote it with college ESL students in mind, but it can also be used with any basic writers, including native speakers of English, high school students, middle school students, and adult education students. Anyone who has not yet developed fluency in writing and/or reading, and therefore is finding academic reading and writing difficult, will benefit from the approach and activities herein. The book is not for beginning ESL students; ESL students who use the book should have some basic knowledge of English. A second book in this series, *Achieving Clarity in English*, helps students to develop fluent and clear academic writing. Accompanying the books is a teacher reference book, *Guide to Fluency First: A Whole-Language Approach*, with chapters on the theoretical bases for a whole-language approach, the Fluency First curriculum, and many ideas for helping students to develop their reading and writing abilities.

In *Achieving Fluency in English*, I ask students to write a 10,000 word "book", do daily freewriting, read 1,000 pages of fiction, respond in journals, and work in small writing and reading groups in class to better understand their readings and to improve their written pieces. Through these activities, students achieve fluency: confidence, comfort and control in writing and reading. They learn to write pieces that are comprehensible, logical, complete and interesting to read. They learn to revise their own writing and to help others revise theirs. And they learn to bring their own questions to what they are reading, as well as to develop their knowledge of vocabulary, syntax, spelling, and of how written English flows, all on a highly individualized basis. Further, due to so much exposure to English, they augment their knowledge of the mechanics and grammar of English, without any exercises or correcting...almost effortlessly.

Activities in this book enable students to write expressively, and to write letters and interesting stories, as well as to develop fluency. The book a student writes can be an autobiography, a fictional autobiography, a novel, a magazine, or "The Collected Works of _____ ". Or it can be a combination of some of these. The massive exposure to English afforded by this approach to literacy helps students' oral skills as well, and their critical thinking abilities. But above all, it dramatically augments and accelerates the development of their reading and writing abilities, because it immerses them in pleasurable, real literacy activities, requires that they do a lot of them, and postpones the need for correctness until they are fluent. And in the process, they become increasingly correct by learning at the point of need.

ACKNOWLEDGMENTS

I wish to acknowledge the contributions to this book by the teachers and students in the ESL department at the City College of New York. The teachers' creative approaches to and enthusiasm for whole language learning have made the approach exciting and successful beyond our expectations, and the students' work at creating wonderful books and magazines has taught us a great deal about language learning. In particular, I wish to thank my colleagues, Prof. Betsy Rorschach, a participant of the National Writing Project, and Anthea Tillyer, for the many practical things I have learned from them about the teaching of writing.

To help my students achieve fluency in writing, I have them write expressively and tell stories. In so doing, I have frequently consulted four books. The first two are published by the Teachers and Writers Collaborative. Karen M. Hubert's book, *Teaching and Writing Popular Fiction: Horror, Adventure, Mystery and Romance* provides ideas to help students write in those genres; Meredith Sue Willis' book, *Personal Fiction Writing: A guide to writing from real life* provides numerous ideas to help students to write fiction and to write from their own knowledge. Published by Heinemann are *Creating the Story* by Rebecca Rule and Susan Wheeler, an excellent guide to storytelling; and *Turning Memories into Memoirs* by Denis Ledoux, with many good ideas for telling and interpreting life stories . Many of these authors' ideas appear in this book. I am also indebted to Nancie Atwell for her many ideas on whole language materials, organization, activities, assessment and theory in her book, my favorite resource, *In the Middle*, also published by Heinemann.

Over the past several years, my colleagues and I at CCNY have trained hundreds of teachers in the Fluency First approach, and during those numerous workshops I have gotten many useful ideas from many talented teachers. Several of those ideas are also in this book, but I cannot say whose they are since it's hard to remember where one gets good ideas when one gets so many of them. So I simply want to say "Thank you, my whole-language colleagues, for your help with this book".

Finally, I wish to thank my husband, Ed, for copy-editing the manuscript and providing moral support throughout the project, and my children, Luda and Natasha, for their patience and help.

INTRODUCTION
TO THE STUDENT

Learning to read and write fluently are the goals of this book. Reading fluently means reading at a normal pace and understanding most of what you read without relying on a dictionary. Writing fluently means writing with comfort, control and confidence, and using writing to express yourself, to tell stories, to discover ideas, to think, and to learn. To achieve fluency in writing and reading, you have to do a lot of both. The more you read and write, the more reading and writing will become almost as effortless as speaking.

To become fluent, you will have to stop worrying about being perfect. Just as you made a lot of mistakes learning to speak when you were a child, you will make mistakes in reading and writing. It's normal, and it even helps you to learn. If you had waited to speak your language perfectly before speaking it when you were a child, you would never have learned to speak it. So don't expect perfection when you're reading and writing.

When you begin to write, it will be slow, and you will worry about mistakes. But you shouldn't. Be concerned mainly about getting a lot down on paper, making sense, and writing things that are interesting and important to you. As you keep focused on these things, many of your mistakes will start to take care of themselves, just as they did when you were a child learning to speak. The same is true with reading. As you read the novels, just focus on meaning and trying to understand what's going on. You don't need to know every word or everything written. Just the really important things.

In using this book, you will read 1,000 pages of fiction. That may seem like a lot, but it is only ten pages a day over one semester. At the end of so much reading, you will be a much better reader than you are now, and you will write better and have a larger vocabulary, too. You will also write a 10,000 word book. That, too, may seem like a lot. But it only amounts to four or five pages a week during the semester, which is not hard to produce, especially since you will have a lot of class time to work on your writing.

You will experiment with different kinds of writing, and will work with your classmates to try to improve your writing and theirs. Together you will also discuss the books you will read in order to understand them better. The class will be like a workshop where you get together with others to work hard at the craft of writing, and to understand more of what you read than you probably would working on your own. This book will basically be a reference, a resource, a place to go for ideas to stimulate writing, so that you may enjoy your work, and become a creative writer as well.

The philosophy behind this "Fluency First" approach is that reading and writing, which are language activities, can be acquired in ways similar to the way in which oral language is acquired: through abundant, important, meaning-driven practice. You will take yourself seriously as an author and read appreciatively and critically. And you will progress greatly if you do the recommended quantity of work, participate fully, work hard, and take risks.

This is not a grammar approach, where correctness is the main concern, but one in which you must strive for fluency by making and negotiating meaning. Nonetheless, you **will learn** a great deal of grammar, probably more than you would in a grammar course, as you read a thousand pages of popular fiction, containing tens of thousands of grammatically correct sentences and well developed paragraphs. You will read no misspelled words, and everything you read will be correctly punctuated. You will develop a strong sense of syntax and an extensive vocabulary as a result of all of your reading. And as you work to produce the substantial amount of writing that is suggested in the text, you will learn even more about grammar, syntax, spelling and vocabulary by experimenting with the language, by teaching yourself, and by asking teachers and peers for help. Studying grammar sequentially does not necessarily help students to achieve correctness. The research on such teaching and on correcting students' papers shows these activities to be largely a waste of time, and suggests that they may actually hinder students' progress in writing.

Your teacher will help you with grammar and the mechanics of writing whenever you have a question, as well as when your writing becomes fluent and you are ready to edit. But don't worry about editing or correctness now. Focus on the more important task in writing - composing - and take risks while writing, which we all must do in order to become good writers. As you compose, you will likely ask many grammar questions, and when a teacher answers them, you will learn and remember more grammar. Once you have worked hard on writing a piece, drafting and redrafting it until it is fluent and interesting, you will then both produce more correct pieces than you would if you were trying to compose and edit at the same time. That is, you will be better able to use the knowledge of grammar that you have learned in grammar-based courses to edit your own work. In essence, the process of composing first and editing later helps students do both better.

In class, students will help each other. At first, you will work with partners, listening to each others' written pieces and helping each other to improve them. After a few weeks, you will share your written pieces with your small group of 5, and get their reactions to each piece of your book. This will help you to hear your piece as others hear it. Then you will revise your written pieces with their responses in mind.

You will also respond to the novels you are reading by writing in double-entry journals, and then discussing your responses with your peers. The journals will enable you to bring your own questions and observations to bear on the text, and to comprehend and appreciate as much as possible. Rather than have the teacher asking you the traditional comprehension questions, this approach allows you to enter into the text and to enjoy it, yet be critical of it, as you might enjoy discussing and critiquing a movie or play you have seen. When students can control this discussion, they learn the most. Reading groups will be comprised of 5 students. In these groups you will read out loud your written reactions to the book being read, and then the group members will respond to what you have said. These discussions will help you all to understand the plot and characters much better.

A whole language classroom looks like a place where real newspapers or books are published, where writers work on their pieces, drafting, consulting with peers, and revising pieces until they are fluent (logical, complete, understandable), and as interesting as possible; and where readers read and respond to what they read. Your class will be like a workshop rather than a traditional teacher-centered class with students progressing through the same material at the same pace. In such a workshop, you will exercise a great deal of choice.

Teachers will take small amounts of class time for short instructional demonstrations, discussions of problems the class may be having, or discussing the chapters in this book or your novels. Teachers will also demonstrate helpful writing and reading behaviors and techniques. For example, the class might watch a small group and the teacher discuss a book, revise a piece after reading it aloud to a group for advice, or use a computer. Then the class will discuss the processes of the activities they have been observing. Teachers will also teach reactively every day because students will ask many questions. And teachers might even share their own writing with the class. But otherwise, teachers will probably spend most class time helping groups, responding to individual students' questions, conferring with you about the content and fluency of your pieces, and keeping track of your work. This approach will help you to do something you must do as a learner -teach yourself - because you will be learning what you uniquely need to learn when you are most receptive to do so. Have you ever sat in a class or read a textbook assignment that was either too easy (boring) or too much over your head (frustrating)? In both cases, you probably wasted a lot of precious time.

4

In the Fluency First approach you will learn far more than before. But I must warn you. At first, you will feel overburdened by how much reading and writing are expected of you. Then, after a few weeks, you will be able to do much more reading and writing in shorter periods of time, and you will enjoy both much more. So don't give up if the work seems too much for you at first. Read the following to prepare yourself for the course.

REGULAR CLASS ACTIVITIES

1. daily freewriting in your writing journal;
2. reading a minimum of ten pages a day, seven days a week;
3. writing a double-entry reading journal;
4. helping and being helped by peers in writing and reading:
5. doing a writing project;
6. revising everything you write for the writing project;
7. conferring with the teacher on a regular basis.

MATERIALS YOU WILL NEED FOR WRITING

1. A loose leaf binder and plenty of loose leaf paper
2. Tabs, erasable pens, transparent tape and scissors

TIPS FOR SUCCESS

1. Keep up with the work. DON'T PROCRASTINATE!
2. Don't be afraid to use your imagination. In fact, use it to the hilt.
3. Be active in class, especially in your discussion groups. Ask for help whenever you need it, and help others when they seek you out.
4. If you have access to a computer, use it to write your book. It's much easier to revise and edit your pieces on a computer.
5. Think of your class as a literacy club which you have joined to have a good time and to improve yourself. Be as active in that club as you would in any other. Then you'll be really pleased.

CHAPTER ONE

FREEWRITING

You are going to freewrite every day for ten minutes. This will help you to become comfortable with writing and to write important and interesting things. It will also help you to produce the 10,000 words you'll need for the book you write.

Think for a few minutes of something you'd like to talk about on paper. If you can't think of anything, choose one of the themes below. Then write about it for ten minutes WITHOUT STOPPING. It is important not to stop when you begin freewriting. It helps you to see that you can actually write a lot in a short amount of time, and to not be worried about making mistakes. If you make a mistake, just cross it out and keep going. Sample topics:

1. How my parents met and fell in love
2. The day I was born
3. How I want to be remembered after I die

Once you start to freewrite, try not to stop for the entire ten minutes. If you don't, you will probably fill up an entire page, or maybe even two. The reason for not stopping is to prove to yourself that you can write a lot in a short period of time...you do have a lot to say!

After freewriting, skip a few lines at the end of your piece, and just write a sentence or two about how you felt when you were freewriting.

SHARING

Now, turn to a partner and read aloud what you have written. Sit next to your partner, so that s/he can read along silently with you. After you have done so, your partner will read his/her piece aloud to you. Then tell each other what you liked or found interesting about each others' pieces.

SHARING WITH THE CLASS

The teacher will ask you to share with the class how you felt as you did your first freewrite. She may also ask for a few students to read their pieces aloud to the whole class. Don't feel embarrassed to share; it helps you to write better and to revise better. It helps you to realize, too, that writing is meant to be read.

IDEAS FOR FUTURE FREEWRITES

Next, close your eyes and think of things, people, places and events in your life that you remember vividly. As you think of each one, write their names and a word or short phrase on the lines on the following page, words that will help you to remember those topics later. Then you can refer to this list for topics for future freewrites. After you write each one, close your eyes again and think back, or think of your life now, and about the interesting, or exciting, or troubling events that have influenced your life or perhaps changed its course, and people that you've liked, loved or hated. Think of places you love, dreams you've had, laughs you've had, fears, traumas, scares, embarrassing moments, troubles, tragedies, adventures, and other things that you remember or know well. Write them as you think of them.

MEMORIES

BRAINSTORMED IDEAS
FOR FREEWRITES

      In order to have even more topics to consider for freewriting, the class will brainstorm together, suggesting topics that would make for good freewrites. The teacher will write these on the board, and you should write down on the lines below any topics that appeal to you, to have even more interesting topics to choose from.

_____

_____

_____

_____

_____

_____

_____

_____

_____

_____

_____

_____

_____

_____

_____

_____

_____

_____

_____

On the next page are other suggested areas for future freewrites. Refer to these pages if you are uninspired during freewrite.

MORE IDEAS FOR FREEWRITES

My opinion about (anything)
What I'm learning in my _____ course
How I feel about life
My (or someone else's) worst flaw
My mother (or) My father
The latest gossip
What I learned from _____
My worst day
A move I made
A special place
A love story
My worries
God
Life after death
My ideals
Sickness
Money and me
My worst fear
A person or place I hate
A person who hates me
When I became a teenager
When I felt like an outsider
My home
Where I grew up
My days as a child
My early school days
Men
Women
A time I failed
My native country

Someone who hurt me
Friends
My insecurities
People I admire
What I'm really like
Going to college
Difficulties I'm having
Growing up
Working
Getting married
Having children
Family problems
Being single
Overcoming problems/handicaps
Learning English
Learning to write
My imaginings
If I were rich...
My greatest ambition(s)
A scary event
A romance
An adventure
A memorable conversation
Being thin/heavy/tall/short
Being young
Growing old
Me and learning
Being different
Where I like most to be
A drinking story
A party story

Growing old
Me and learning
Being different
Where I like most to be
A drinking story
A party story
Me and self control
Me and saving
A great moment in sports
Violence I've seen
A conflict in my life
A time I helped others
Music in my life
A death that affected me
A war story
Advice to my children
Unfairness
The important things in life
Home
Dreams that have troubled me
Food and me
The coming millennium
A hundred years from now
Dancing and me
A funny story
What people's faces reveal
Today...
Yesterday...
Tomorrow...
My enemies
A person I remember vividly
People I've hurt and why
People who have hurt me & why

Why I _____
A great story
What I don't understand
Where I've been happiest
Present challenges
What life means to me
An experience that changed the
way I think about myself,
another, or life
How I plan to achieve
happiness
Trouble I've been in and why
How I want to be remembered;
How I'd write my eulogy
How I want to affect people,
and why
Places I dream of going or
living
Talk at the dinner table when I
was growing up
Things my family did together
What friends have taught me
What I've learned from living
What I think about dying and
an afterlife
How my family thought about
things
What my family valued and
believed
How my family interacted and
behaved

What I remember most about
  my childhood: smells,
  sounds, faces, places,
  words, animals, favorite
  activities, traumas, my
  room, my things, school
How I think the world should
  be run and people should
  behave
What my mother, father,
  grandmother,
grandmother, etc. always
used to say
Leaving friends, country,
  culture, home, family to
  come to the U.S.A.
What I think about capital
  punishment
What I think about abortion
What I think about euthanasia
What I think about capitalism
  compared with socialism
What I think about republicans
  vs. democrats
What I think about Americans
What I would do differently if I
  could live my life over
  again
The greatest game/movie/show
  I have ever seen
Where I want to be in 25 years
Letter to an editor

What I would do if I were
  president of the U.S.A.
The one I love
The meanest or weirdest or
  most depressed or most
  outrageous person I know
The most important things I've
  learned in life
A great love scene
A fight I've been in (physical
  or verbal) or witnessed
How I or my opponent saw
  that fight
The rupture caused by the
  fight and how it affected
  my relationship with him
  or her
A time I did something sneaky,
  or dishonest
What I look like
How my parents see (or saw)
  the world
A flashback
My first date
My first marriage
My years as a football,
  baseball, basketball, or
  hockey player
Holidays and my family
Writing and me
A story or fable my parents
  used to tell to teach a
  moral

POINT-OF-VIEW FREEWRITES

One of the most enjoyable ways to freewrite is to write as if you were someone else: a character in a book, a political figure, a religious leader, a movie star, a sports hero, a war hero, an historical figure (king, queen, slave, caveman/cavewoman, explorer, etc.), an animal, an inanimate object, your mother, your father, a friend or a relative, a crazy person, a doctor, a person from another country or culture, or just about anyone.

From this other point of view, you could write a letter, a speech, a diary entry, a challenge, a report of what happened, an essay, a poem, a song, a threat, a monologue saying what's on your mind, a prayer, an inaugural address, a critique, a sermon, or whatever you wish. You have considerable artistic freedom since you are someone else writing.

You could write a letter from someone in the past to those living now, or to another person from the past. You could write to your future children, or to ancient ancestors. You could write your secrets, or unfold a mystery. You could write messages from a military leader of the past. Or you could explain how it was to live in a certain era in the past.

You could write a letter from Christopher Columbus to present-day Americans, or from your great-great grandparents to yourself. You could write a news report in the year 2100, or how it feels to be growing inside the womb. You could write to someone in the past and point out how he or she should have done things differently. On the following page are more suggestions. Point-of-view writing is really fun and allows you to be very creative.

MORE SUGGESTIONS FOR
POINT OF VIEW FREEWRITES

A letter from your stomach or your heart to you
A diary entry your first girlfriend/boyfriend may have made
A speech your mother would make if she were president
A sermon you would make if you were a preacher/priest/rabbi
What a baby would say if he/she could talk to you
What a murderer for hire says to himself
What you would write in a chapter about history during your life
Your report as a psychiatrist of someone's behavior and problems
A telephone conversation two world leaders might have
What you feel like as a blind person
Diary entries some famous person may have made
Letters from leaders of warring countries to each other
An interior monologue of a person getting ready for an important event
An interior monologue of a person on his/her first date with someone
A description of you as someone else sees you
A letter Jesus or Mohammed or Moses would write to people of today
A dialogue between two famous people of today or from the past

On the following page are some sample openers. Use your imagination and finish the paragraphs. Don't worry about correctness; just concentrate on trying to write interesting things. Try to be the character from whose point of view you are writing. Just write a few sentences for each starter to see how it feels; then share your work with classmates to see who has been the most inventive. I think you'll find out that point-of-view freewriting can be very entertaining.

1. Most people don't understand what it's like to be a dog. But as a dog, I

_____

_____

_____

_____

_____

_____

2. You might remember me. My name is Abraham Lincoln. I'd like to tell
you why _____ _____

_____

_____

_____

_____

_____

3. Movie stars like myself are so misunderstood. People think _____

_____

_____

_____

_____

_____

4. Living on Mars is far different from what earthlings believe. We
Martians _____

_____

_____

_____

_____

_____

CHAPTER TWO

READING & RESPONDING TO NOVELS

1,000 PAGES OF FICTION

You and your classmates will read several novels this semester, for a total of about 1,000 pages of reading. This may seem like a lot to you, especially if you haven't read much in the past. But it's only about 10 pages a day for one semester. And you need to read this extensively to become fluent in English, both in the written and oral language. As you read so much, reading becomes more and more automatic, thus less and less difficult. Your vocabulary increases, your spelling improves, your understanding of grammar and idiomatic usage advance, all without much effort because reading novels is fun.

Novels tell interesting stories, and introduce us to fascinating people. They relate how these people live, love, think, feel, and often, die. They tell of their adventures, their mistakes, and their problems. They give us a lot of experience not only in understanding people and their problems, but in understanding the language, and how to tell a good story. Your teacher may choose the novels you will read or ask the class to choose them. What's important is that they will be entertaining and not too difficult to read. Reading them will also help you to write interesting stories during this course. Or you may even choose to write a novel for your 10,000 word project. Many of my students have written pretty good ones.

You will do some reading in class, especially when you begin a new novel. And the teacher will occasionally read aloud as you read silently. Sometimes, you will just read silently. But each time you meet with your class, you will discuss what you're reading in small groups (4 to 5), and with the whole class as well.

These discussions will be like talking with a friend about a movie you two have just seen. You don't have to analyze the whole reading, just talk about what you liked, what you didn't like, what you didn't understand, and other normal responses to something that interests or entertains you. To help you prepare for these discussions, you should do the following:

1. **Write at the top of every page you read a word, phrase, a sentence or a summary to help you remember what happened on that page.**

2. **Highlight or underline vocabulary that you do not understand; then when you meet with your reading group, ask them (or your teacher) what the words mean.**

3. **Keep a reading journal on lined loose-leaf paper. Your journal entries will be the basis for class discussions. When your class is reading a new novel, for each class meeting, write 2 questions about the reading; 2 quotes from the book (parts that you thought were important or that you really liked); and 10 new words that you think are important.**

After discussing the first few chapters with these types of notes, you will begin a double-entry journal. This will take a little more time. Journal pages will have a line drawn vertically down the middle of each page, with material copied directly from the novel on the left side, and your own written reactions to the material on the right. You will decide what to copy and what responses you will make.

DOUBLE-ENTRY READING JOURNALS

Your reactions may include questions, challenges, opinions, analogies, inferences you make, musings, or conclusions you draw from the reading. Initially, your teacher will give you time in class to do double-entry journals, so that she and your peers will be able to help you get used to writing them. After you can do them on your own, they will be a regular homework assignment.

On the following page is a sample double-entry journal page. Notice how the page is divided by a vertical line down the middle, and that the left side has copied parts, while the right side has the reader's responses. And notice that these are a reader's own responses, not answers to a teacher's questions; and that they include opinions, questions, inferences, interpretations, and musings. That is, the reader is talking back to the book as she writes her responses.

Each day, when you get together with your group in class, you will read your journal entries to each other - copied parts and responses - and then discuss what each of you reads. This will help your group to understand the plot and the vocabulary, as well as the characters and their motivations.

As you write your journal entries, also make a list of the vocabulary that is new to you in the readings. Then when you meet with your group, you will be able to find out the meanings, and use this new vocabulary in your discussions and writings about the book. That way your vocabulary will be constantly increasing. You are not limited to a certain amount of words; just write words that are new for you.

DOUBLE-ENTRY JOURNAL SAMPLE

(from <u>The</u> <u>Great</u> <u>Gilly</u> <u>Hopkins</u>, by Katharine Peterson)

COPIED	RESPONSES
"My name, Gilly said, is Galadriel."	*She sounds very sure of herself, and angry.*
"But I am not nice. I am brilliant. I am famous across the entire country. Nobody wants to tangle with the Great Gilly Hopkins. I am too clever and too hard to manage. Gruesome Gilly, they call me."	*Gilly sounds very angry and mean. She also sounds like she thinks she's better than anyone else. She has probably hurt a lot of people. I wonder why. Maybe because she's angry about being in foster care. Or maybe she has been abused.*
"Well, 'scuse me honey," Mame Trotter said.	*I would not have been as polite as Mrs. Trotter if a new kid had corrected me so rudely.*
"You belong here now."	*Mrs. Trotter is really trying to make Gilly feel loved.*
"Well, we been needing somebody to rearrange the dust around here, ain't we?"	*Mrs. Trotter even forgave Gilly for being rude and dusting the bench before she sat down. She's really a loving person.*
Gilly gave William Ernest the most fearful face in all her repertory of scary looks. *She could stand anything, as long as she was in charge.*	*Gilly was so mean. What makes big kids bully little ones? I've never understood that.* *Gilly wants to control everyone, even adults. But why?*

The reason for double-entry journals is that they allow you to pick out the parts you think are important, and to ask the questions that you have, rather than do exercises a teacher makes up. Doing your reading this way will help to improve your comprehension and vocabulary.

SPEAKING OF VOCABULARY

You don't have to understand every word you read. If you are reading and you understand the story line, but do not understand some of the words, you can infer the meanings of those words from the context you read them in. And so, just by reading, you will learn new words without too much trouble. And if you try to use them when writing, you'll remember them even better.

I like students to write the new words in their journals, then ask me or a peer for the meanings in class - especially of words that seem very important to the story line. I also like students to try to use the new vocabulary words in their discussions and in their writings. This helps them to sink in.

You and your classmates and teacher should collaboratively choose 25 to 50 so new words each week that you all agree are important, and that you will all be responsible to learn, words that are used frequently and are new for most of the class. You should study these with classmates and alone. And you should try to use them in your written pieces. Good vocabulary makes writing more specific and alive.

Now take a book you are reading and write double entries on the next page. Your reactions can begin with words like, "For me,..." "I think...", "I like...", "I don't understand...", "I'm confused about...", "This reminds me of...", "Why did...? and so on. Afterwards, read your entries to your group, listen to theirs, and respond freely. You'll see that these entries will give you a lot to talk about in your group.

DOUBLE ENTRY JOURNAL

COPIED   **RESPONSES**

_____
_____
_____
_____
_____
_____
_____
_____
_____
_____
_____
_____
_____
_____
_____
_____
_____
_____
_____
_____
_____
_____
_____
_____
_____
_____
_____

TIPS FOR READING

In class

You will be reading in class (along with your teacher or alone), alone outside of class, and with peers in places like the library. Look over the following suggestions for getting the most out of your reading in all three circumstances.

When the teacher reads aloud in class and you read along silently, it helps you to learn sound-spelling correspondences in English. It also helps you learn how to chunk, i.e. to read in syntactic or thought groups. And it helps you to read fast enough that you will not lose the meaning. If you read too slow, you will not keep up with the story line very well. Finally, it helps you to learn how to stress the important words in English sentences, and so it will improve your speaking. So be very attentive when your teacher reads aloud. Also, ask the teacher meanings you are not getting as she reads, rather than at the end.

With others

One of the biggest favors you can do for yourself is to study with a group of classmates outside of class time. The library is a good place, or someone's home, or even the cafeteria. Try to get a group together to study and do homework. As you read and write with your peers, and discuss both what you're reading and writing, your English skills will improve greatly, and you'll be making friends as well. And if you can't do this, at least have a phone partner that you can call and collaborate with over homework assignments. Two heads are better than one!

On your own

When you read alone, find a quiet, comfortable place to read, one with good lighting. Many people like to bring the novels they're reading to the beach, or park, or even on the subway or bus. But you have to be able to block out the noise in those places. You can also read before sleeping. But most important, try to read regularly: 10 pages a day is recommended for this course. Set aside about an hour each day, seven days a week, to read. Look at the weekly schedule on the next page and try to block out one hour per day for reading your novels. Then put your schedule in a place where you will see it to remind you when to read each day.

	SUN	MON	TUES	WEDS	THUR	FRI	SAT
a.m.							
p.m.							

Audio-visual aids

Many of the books we read have been made into movies. Watching them as we read is not only beneficial, it also makes the reading come alive and can be very exciting. Your teacher will probably select or suggest books with accompanying movies. There are also companies like Recorded Books that have audiotapes to accompany the books. These tapes really help comprehension. Just be sure to use unabridged versions, which say the same as the book.

TAKE A POINT OF VIEW

Activity 1

Take the part of one of the characters during group discussions, and speak as if you really were that character. Speaking from his or her point of view, you can talk about the plot, your underlying motives and feelings, your relationships with other characters, and more. It is a really enjoyable way to discuss the books, and to understand them.

Activity 2

Write some pieces as if you were that character. The first one will be a piece introducing yourself, but without revealing your name. Write a physical self-description, explain your feelings, and your version of what is going on in the book. Your teacher will hang up all the pieces around the room, and the everyone will read all the pieces and have to figure out which character each is written by.

Activity 3

Next you will write a letter from your character to another character in the book, trying to straighten out a problem (describe the problem, analyze it, and recommend a solution), or to explain why it can't be straightened out.

Activity 4

Write a letter telling your side of the story. Tell how the other characters have misunderstood or perhaps maligned you. Write in self defense, analyzing your behaviors and values, and explain how/if you would change things if you could, and why you are right. You will give that piece to that character, await his/her written reply, and write back until you two have straightened out the problem.

CHAPTER THREE

LEARNING WITH OTHERS

To learn a language, you have to interact with others. Likewise, to understand books you're reading as well as academic subjects, it is best if you talk your way through the material with other students: asking your own questions, trying to explain things in your own words, and quizzing each other on what you're learning. This helps you to remember more. And to improve your writing, you must read it to others and find out what they think. This means that you must work with others. In doing so, you will help them to learn and they will help you. You will also be helping yourself to learn. But since lots of people are shy, we'll first try to break the ice.

Icebreaker activity #1

If you haven't yet met a friend in class, you will today. Take a few minutes and introduce yourself to the person next to you. Then interview that person and find out as many interesting, memorable things about them as possible. Take notes so that you will remember as much as possible. Then let the person interview you. When you are finished, the teacher will put all the students in a big circle and you will each introduce the person you interviewed. As each student speaks, take notes on what s/he says. Try to remember as much as possible about each student, especially their names, and one or two interesting things about them. At the end of the introductions, the teacher will quiz the group on each student that was introduced.

Icebreaker activity #2

Now read to a partner the freewrite you did for today. Then your partner will write on your piece the thing(s) s/he noticed the most; then s/he will sign it. Then listen to your partner's piece and respond in like manner.

Icebreaker activity #3

Now you and your partner will get out your reading journals and read to each other the questions, quotations, responses and new words you wrote for the day. As you do this, feel free to discuss the book. Help each other to understand new vocabulary. Ask the teacher or a peer for the meanings of words you don't know. And take notes as you discuss the book (e.g. write meanings of words).

Icebreaker activity #4

Your teacher will put the class in groups of 5. Sit with your group in a circle, and introduce yourselves again. One student will be the group leader, and the rest of you will be characters in the book you are reading. Then you will discuss what's going on in the book, and how you feel about it, as if you were that character.

Icebreaker activity #5

With your group of five, read the next chapter or pages of the novel assigned by your teacher. Have the student with the best accent read it aloud while the rest follow along. Stop whenever you have a question or a comment, but keep going until you have finished the assignment. You will be amazed at how much you learn. Then plan to meet outside of class to study, to do the next reading assignment. When you meet, do the same. And try to set up a regular meeting time to read, write and study together.

Icebreaker activity #6

With a partner, discuss and then choose the roles of two characters in a book you are reading. Then silently, write on the same paper a dialogue between the two characters as if you were they. You might have an argument, question each other about motives, discuss another character or an event in the book, or tell each other why you have behaved as you have. The only rule is that you cannot talk.

Icebreaker activity #7

Your teacher will assign you the role of a character in the book you are reading, and specify a character that you are to write a letter to. Write the letter, discussing what's going on in the book or what's on your mind, and either challenge, make assertions about, or ask the other character questions. The teacher will give your letter to that character, and she or he will write back to you. Keep corresponding until you have come to an agreement or an understanding with the other character.

Icebreaker activity #8

With your group, make an appointment to meet in the cafeteria, library, or elsewhere to study together for one hour or more. When you meet, have one of the group members record in writing what you discussed or studied during your meeting.

Icebreaker activity #9

With your group, discuss and draw up some guidelines you should adhere to as you work together, whether discussing readings or listening to and making observations about each others' writing. Then write these up and have a group member report them to the class.

RULES FOR WORKING EFFECTIVELY IN GROUPS

As each group reports on activity #9, the teacher will write all the suggestions on the board. Then the class will discuss them and agree on the ones that are most important. Remember to be positive.

In General

_____
_____
_____
_____
_____

During Discussions of Readings

_____
_____
_____
_____
_____

During Discussions of Written Pieces

_____
_____
_____
_____
_____

Now write below how you felt the first time the teacher asked you to read aloud to other students something you had written .

_____
_____
_____
_____
_____

Write how you feel now that you have read several of your pieces aloud to other students.

_____
_____
_____
_____
_____

Write why you think the teacher wants you to read your pieces to others, and what might be the advantages of doing so.

_____
_____
_____
_____
_____

You will share these reactions with the class.

Icebreaker activity #10

Spend twenty minutes freewriting two paragraphs, and using the following openings: in paragraph #1, "I used to be ...."; and in paragraph #2, "But now I ...." Once you have finished, read it silently to yourself and make any revisions you wish.

When everyone's finished, the class will sit in a full circle. Everyone (including the teacher) will read their pieces to the whole class, and the rest will listen. After each piece has been read, those listening will write down one observation about the piece - not a criticism, nor a compliment, nor a suggestion. Just write down an observation: something you noticed, something that stood out in the piece. After a piece has been read aloud, one by one everyone will read their observations aloud to the author; the author should listen and take notes for possible revisions later on.

Write now what you think are some good responses you can make after you listen to a fellow student read a piece.

_____
_____
_____
_____

Brainstorm your responses with the class and add some more below. Remember, you are like fellow authors helping each other to be creative and interesting.

_____
_____
_____
_____

CHAPTER FOUR

DEVELOPING THE CRAFT OF WRITING

In this course, you will write life stories and creative ones. To make them interesting and memorable, you must work hard to turn your memories into memoirs, and make your stories ones your readers will want to hear over and over. So you must work at the craft of writing. A craft is something you work on with your hands and mind and imagination and emotions. So in this class/workshop, you and your classmates will work seriously on the craft of writing every day. Your teachers and peers will help you to make your writing better, but you will make most of the decisions about your own writing, just as you would about a painting you were working on or anything else you were making.

WHAT IS WRITING? HOW DOES IT DEVELOP?

First, let's talk about what writing is. It's very important that you understand what writing is and what it is not. Writing is not a matter of pleasing teachers, avoiding errors, being neat, or torturing yourself. Nor is writing something that only a few people can do well. Writing is a language and thinking process, which ends with a written product, and you can be just as successful learning to write as you were in learning to speak your native language.

You learned your native language by using it extensively: listening, speaking, experimenting with new words and constructions, and even playing with language. You acquired it naturalistically and through massive exposure and practice. And you did it by concentrating mainly on the **meaning** you were trying to convey or grasp, doing this for years, controlling the process yourself, yet with lots of interaction with others, and not worrying about making mistakes along the way.

Writing and reading are also best learned in ways similar to oral language. The difference between writing and speaking is that what you put down on paper is the **only** thing that your readers have; that is, they must grasp your intended meaning or follow your ideas from only what you have written. You will likely not be next to them to clarify things if they do not understand. And even if your writing is of a conversational or informal nature, it will not be the same as a real conversation. So it must be as clear as possible.

Writing is generally far more succinct than talking. A good way to appreciate this is to tape-record a conversation or a monologue and then try to write it down. First of all, there are no gestures, facial expressions or intonation to help you understand the written text. Second, there will be many false starts, interjections, corrections, and repetitions in the written transcript. But writing does not have these supports. Thus the writer's full meaning must be in the text he or she writes.

A popular misconception about writing is that very few people can learn to write well. **Anyone** can learn to write well by **working hard** at it, **getting others' help** and **persevering.** You must also **trust yourself** that you have interesting and informative things to say. And you must write with the same conviction and energy that you use when you talk. Your readers should not only read what you think, but hear **your voice**...the unique way you have of expressing yourself. That's what gives life and authenticity to a piece.

RULES FOR WRITERS' WORKSHOP

Since you will be writing a good deal in class, the following rules explain how you must work at writing in class (adapted from Nancie Atwell, *In the Middle*, Boynton-Cook, 1988). Review them carefully.

1. There should be no erasing. You should save your thoughts because maybe you'll want to use them again. Just draw one line through anything you might ordinarily erase.

2. Write on one side of the paper only (except for journal writing). Then you may cut up your piece and reorganize it, pasting the pieces in a different order.

3. Save everything you write, because in this course, you will become a writer, and it's necessary to understand your own processes of writing and not to throw out gems by mistake.

4. Date and label everything you write. e.g. Mystery story, draft #2, March 5. Or "notes" 4/3, "research summaries" 11/2.

5. Speak quietly when you work with partners. It's important for you and your classmates to be able to think as you plan, write, revise and edit. You can't do that if others' noise is distracting you.

6. Work really hard. Pretend that writing is your livelihood. That will make you work hard on your pieces.

LIFE STORIES

START WITH LISTS

Make a comprehensive list of the events, decisions, and relationships that have shaped your life, things like births, illnesses, deaths, moves, fires, tornados, floods, famines, accidents, the community you grew up in, the religion you were raised in, your important relationships (romantic, or with relatives, friends, teachers, employers), a failure or success, love relationships, marriage, children, career choices, spiritual experiences. Write these below.

_____

_____

_____

_____

_____

_____

_____

_____

_____

_____

_____

_____

_____

_____

_____

_____

Next, group all the items that can be grouped under an appropriate heading.

_____ _____ _____ _____

_____

_____

_____

_____

_____

_____

_____

_____

_____

Now, narrow your list to ten relationships, decisions, or events that have been most crucial, those that made you a different person.

_____

_____

_____

_____

_____

_____

_____

_____

These will probably be the richest source of material for writing your memoirs. You can write about them as whole stories, or write vignettes, scenes, dialogues, or descriptions, all full of details which you remember because these have been so significant to your life.

FAMILY STORIES

These will come easily. These are stories you have told before, probably more than once. They might have happened on family vacations, or when you were little, or at the dinner table, or on the beach, or during a family party or disagreement. Take a mental photo of the event, and describe the details: Who was there? Where were they? What were they doing, wearing, saying? What were the sounds, smells, tastes, textures, feelings, etc. of the scene?

LETTERS TO YOUR FAMILY

Now write letters to someone - alive or dead - as if you were composing a real letter. Ask questions. Share your thoughts and feelings. Then answer your letter as if you were the person you had written to, and answer your questions, sharing your thoughts and feelings as well. Your subconscious will help you out.

WRITE IN YOUR JOURNAL

Write in a private place - a journal, for example - and explore some problem or disturbing memory, issue, loss, or person. Write about difficult things that have caused you pain, but only for as long as you feel comfortable doing so.

DESCRIBE PEOPLE YOU KNOW/KNEW WELL

Do this patiently and in great detail. Use specific, unique details about their looks, their facial expressions, posture, walk, gestures, clothing, activities, talk, feelings, what was important to them, what they thought of others, how they treated others, their daily activities and concerns, their personalities, their flaws, and how they did things, and reacted to events and people, how they lived and how they died.

BEFORE WRITING A STORY, MAKE A LIST

Think of a story that you heard often in childhood. Write a list of the details in it, then write a rough draft. Writing a quick list helps you to write the draft. Or list the five or two or ten most important events in your life, then pick one, write a list of things you see or remember during that event, then write a rough draft.

Think of a person you love or hate. Write a list of descriptive words, things they say, feelings they have, attitudes, habits, preoccupations, how they behave, what they value, what they believe. Then write a vignette of the person in action in a specific scene, and work in some things on your list.

I suggest writing a series of vignettes - or short stories - which capture the most important events, places, people, and issues in your life. Or you may want to combine the story of your life with a political history of your country. Getting started is easy. In the next fifteen minutes, just write on a piece of paper the names, places, and people most prominent in your life, and then write associations you make in thinking about them. For example:

ME AT AGE __: shy, anxious to make friends, skinny...
HOME: Santo Domingo, warm, bare feet, music, my bed, the smell of dinner, blue Caribbean waters, sandy beaches, brothers and sisters
MOTHER: beautiful smile, cleaning, talking with father, caring for baby, listening to me after school, cooking, laughing
THE EARLY YEARS: feeling secure, playing with siblings, best friends, projects, escapades, favorite things, accidents, fears, heroes, heroines, hideouts, dreams, learning to get along with others...
THE TOWN: police, old folks, neighbors, church, school, stores, roads, events, trees and flowers, typical days...
BIRTHDAYS: parties, games, presents, cakes, anticipation...
SCHOOL: favorite people, easy/difficult studies, fears, traumas, happy times, ballgames...

LIFE STORY QUESTIONS

Here are some questions that may guide you in your research for your autobiography or biography. You do not need to write about all of them...just the ones for which you have the best material.

CHILDHOOD

1. What are your earliest memories?
2. What do you remember about grandparents or other relatives?
3. Whom did you spend the most time with? What did you do?
4. Did anyone you were close to die? How did you react?
5. Who was your earliest favorite person?
6. What was your home like?
7. How did your parents deal with you and your siblings?
8. What kinds of games did you play; what toys did you have?
9. Who were your neighbors? Did you have friends?
10. What were your other childhood activities?
11. What were family meals like?
12. What were other family routines?
13. Describe religious training in your home.
14. Describe a momentous event in your childhood.
15. What fears did you have as a child?
16. What were your family's most important ceremonies?
17. What are your fondest early memories?
18. Who did the most/least talking at home?
19. Did your family ever move?
20. What were the family rules for conduct; what was the family philosophy?
21. Were there new babies in your household?
22. Were there elderly relatives? How were they cared for?

23. What happened when you or others became ill?
24. When your parents were out or away, who took care of you?
25. If a parent or a close relative was out of work, who
     helped him or her? Was there outside help from charity
     or the government?
26. What was your room like? Did you have a favorite place?
27. What person do you remember most vividly from childhood?
28. What was school like for you as a child?

YOUR PARENTS

1.   What work did your father and mother do?
2.   Did your parents read and write much? When, what, where?
3.   What did you talk about at the dinner table?
4.   What did your parents say about their work?
5.   Did your parents spend a lot of time with each other? Did
     they talk with each other a lot? About what kinds of things?
6.   What were your parents' priorities?
7.   Did your father and mother have friends? Describe them.
8.   Which parent were you closer to? Explain.
9.   Who made the major decisions in the family?
10. Who took care of the children? And their discipline?
11. What did you like to do with your parents?
12. How old were your parents when they married? What was the
     extent of their education?
13. What conflicts did your parents have?
14. What activities did they participate in outside of the home?
15. What was their attitude about your friends, dating,
     courting, moving out on your own, marrying?
16. How were money issues handled by your parents?
17. What kind of entertainment did your parents go in for?
18. Did you ever see your parents grieving? How did you feel?
19. What do you think your parents did wrong in child rearing?

ADOLESCENCE

1. Were sports important to you?
2. What about music?
3. When did you begin to consider yourself grown up?
4. What were your closest friends like?
5. What did you do together?
6. Discuss what school was like: the work, the people, etc.
7. What was your opinion of yourself as a high-schooler?
8. What were your main extra-curricular activities?
9. If you got in trouble at home or school, what happened?
10. Did your parents want you to pursue a certain occupation?
11. What did you want to be when you grew up?
12. Were you ever treated unjustly, unkindly in school? At home?
13. What were your feelings about the opposite sex then?
14. When did people stop treating you like a child?
15. Were you expected to behave in certain ways around adults? How about when you were around the opposite sex?
16. Did you have a job? What did you do with your earnings?
17. How were you disciplined?
18. When did your siblings or you leave home? Was it traumatic?
19. What were your relations with members of other races, religions, linguistic, ethnic or cultural groups?
20. Were there limitations on how you interacted with them?

YOUR SOCIAL SELF

1. How do you define your social class? Explain.
2. How many years of schooling have you and your family members had? What kind of jobs do you and they have/aspire to?
3. Do you have more schooling than your parents? Your friends?

4. To what ethnic group do you belong? What cultural, and/or linguistic group? How does this identification influence your thinking? What do you know about your family's roots?
5. How do you think other groups in society view your group?
6. What are the stereotypes your group holds of other groups?
7. What kind of problems were/are there in the society in which you grew up? What was/is their effect on you?
8. What kind of education did you have? Did you do well in school? What do you remember about your teachers and learning?
9. Is education important in your social group? What is?
10. What social and geographical mobility do you have?
11. Could you improve or change your social class? Will you?
12. What language(s) do you speak? Read? Write?
13. If you speak more than one language, when, where, with whom do you speak, read, write each language? Explain as fully as possible.
14. What kind of literature did/do you like to read? Why?
15. Are you comfortable interacting with people from other ethnic, cultural and linguistic groups?
16. What historical forces and/or events can help to explain your family's present status and history?
17. What are your family's values and beliefs?
18. Do you still hold onto them?
19. What expectations did/does your family have for you?
20. Have these changed due to outside forces or events?

ADULT LIFE

1. What transitions have you made in your life?
2. When did/will you marry? Where? With what kind of party?
3. How did you meet your spouse? Describe your spouse.
4. Did you need your parents' approval to marry?

5. Did you move out of your parents' house while single?
6. Where/how did you live?
7. Did/will you have children? When? How many?
8. Who takes/took care of your children?
9. Did/do/will you raise your children the way you were raised?
10. What is your household like? Do you own or rent?
11. Did you/your spouse work? Where? When? Doing what?
12. How do/did jobs affect family life?
13. If separated or divorced, when and why did it happen?
14. What are your adult routines, rituals, customs?
15. What is your opinion of people you work with?
16. What are your plans for the future?
17. Do you and your spouse communicate about feelings/hopes?
18. What do you talk about regularly?
19. What kind of time do you spend with your children?
20. What are your hopes, fears, etc. concerning them?
21. What are your religious beliefs and practices?
22. What are the similarities and differences between your parents' values and attitudes, and yours today?
23. What conflicts are you experiencing as an adult?

YOUR PSYCHOLOGICAL SELF

1. What kind of a person are you?
2. What things do you value most?
3. What kind of disposition do you have?
4. What are your basic beliefs?
5. Try to characterize your behaviors.
6. Do you understand yourself?
7. Are you happy, troubled? Why?
8. What is your philosophy of life?
9. How do you see other people? How do they see you?
10. If you could change one thing about yourself, what would it be?

SOME OTHER EASY PIECES TO WRITE

SPORTS

Aside from life stories, a relatively easy piece to write is a sports report ...especially if you like sports. First read a few such pieces from newspapers and magazines to get an idea of how they're written. *Sports Illustrated, Time*, or daily newspapers would be the best sources. Then write a report of a real event that you have witnessed.

To do this, watch the event and even videotape it if possible. Take notes on what happens, who did what and when, keep score, and note the outcome. Then write your report and afterwards speculate in writing as to why things occurred the way they did. Illustrate your report with a scoreboard and/or pictures. And make sure you have covered the five W's: who, what, when, where, why (and how, if important).

ACCIDENTS/DISASTERS/PLAGUES/FAMINES/MURDERS

Reports of others' woes are very popular reading. They make us feel bad, which most of us like to feel. They also probably make us feel good to know that the terrible things in the story didn't happen to us, and because we sympathize with the poor victims in the report, and so we feel better about our own humaneness. In this type of story, it is very important to tell the five W's - who, what, when, where, and why - up front and as succinctly as possible. Often these are followed by eye-witness accounts and gory details, ending with the latest news on the disaster, like relief efforts and plans to help the victims. You might also throw in statistics on similar bad occurrences in the past, or predictions that similar ones will occur.

EDITORIALS

Editorials are usually persuasive and informative at the same time. They give the author's point of view on an issue, event, idea, person, policy, or other subject of public interest, and then argue as forcefully as possible to support that opinion. The argument is usually logical and strong, giving little credence or strength to opposing arguments, which are usually given a token mention. Or you can write letters to editors in response to editorials, either agreeing and adding to the argument, or disagreeing and saying why.

To write forcefully about an issue, make sure first that you have enough material to support your thesis, and recommendations to solve the dilemma or problem you are addressing. Make sure to clearly explain the problem, give your arguments and solutions, and deflect counter-arguments if you can, or at least mention them in a way that makes them seem unimportant in comparison to the facts as you see them.

When you write your letter to the editor, your letter should be brief and to the point. If you are arguing with the editor, state your position and give your arguments succinctly but strongly. And make recommendations. If you like, send it in and see if they print it.

FEATURE STORIES

Feature stories focus on a person, place, event or issue of great public interest, and are informative, rather than argumentative, in nature. They are full of facts, and often include interview material and pictures. They give readers an insider's view, rather than just the straight reporting of the five W's. If focusing on a person, they will include not only information on why that person is famous (or infamous), but personal data, the person's philosophy, other areas of the person's life or work, and so forth.

If focusing on an issue, the story may include three or four pieces, like a report, an interview, illustrations (charts, graphs, etc.), and editorial piece, and a first-person account. Or the feature article may include all of these in one piece.

To get a better sense of feature stories, look at feature sections in popular magazines, like *Time* and *Newsweek*, as well as in other magazines and in newspapers.

SCIENCE/TECHNOLOGY PIECES

Many newspapers and news magazines carry a regular science and technology section, explaining new phenomena or experiments or discoveries in laymen's terms. Often these have to do with space, medical innovations, computers, and other technologies. Read several of these for ideas. Then research a subject you are interested in, take notes on it, and write it up. When you write your science piece, be sure to include basic explanations and illustrations to help your readers understand the piece.

POINT-OF-VIEW AUTOBIOGRAPHIES

A really enjoyable project is to write an autobiography as if you were someone else: a deceased person, a living person about whom you know a lot, or an imaginary person. This is, in my view, the most enjoyable and creative experience in biography writing. It allows you complete artistic freedom, challenges your imagination, and is usually the most entertaining form of biography to read.

In any of these cases, remember, do not write a rambling chronicle of not very unique life events. Write a series of interesting pieces that make the person come alive to the reader.

WRITE ABOUT YOURSELF IN DISGUISE

We all have secrets, some of which we will never tell another soul. Why? Because we're ashamed of them and don't wish to lose others' respect. Maybe we've cheated or stolen or lied or been gluttonous, or had delusions of grandeur, or worse. Maybe we're vain, proud, lazy, or harbor ill feelings toward other people. But we can tell our secrets through characters we create. Some very interesting stories can be told if we change the name to protect our reputations.

In any of these cases, remember, do not write a rambling chronicle of not very unique life events. Write a series of interesting pieces that make the person come alive to the reader.

CHAPTER FIVE

WRITING FICTION

TELLING GOOD STORIES

Good stories have certain things in common. They have a plot with a beginning, a middle, and an end. A *conflict* is stated, a main *character or characters* are introduced, there is *rising tension or action*, perhaps complicating the conflict even more, a *crisis, falling action*, and a *conclusion*. A conflict is a problem; what your characters do or say or what happens to them is the action; the crisis or climax or turning point is where things fell apart or came together in the story.

A good story helps your readers to see your characters, hear them, see the action, and find out or infer the conclusion. The drama of your story entertains your readers...the characters, the action, the setting, the dialogue, the suspense, the familiarity, the strangeness. A good story has specific and striking details, not abstract words and phrases. The words mean exactly what you want your readers to see, hear, smell, taste. And no words are wasted. A good story focuses on only one set of characters, actions and settings, AND it puts your readers right where you want them to be. It has a point of view, or the perspective of the narrator. The climax comes fairly soon; the action is quick, not dragged out. It is written like a vignette, which may or may not make a larger plot, as if in separate "takes" when someone is producing a movie. A good story is all there. When you read it to others, you do not need to explain it. If you do, something is missing and you need to go back and revise it.

STORY SKELETONS

Stories, long or short, have familiar skeletons, ones which readers expect and enjoy. Here are some sample story skeletons:

1. Boy meets girl. They fall in love. A big problem threatens to keep them apart. They fight it. It looks like they are going to lose each other, but in the end, they get together.

2. Country A attacks Country B because it wants to build an empire. It enslaves the inhabitants of country B. Country B patriots form an underground resistance movement. Through many exploits of bravery, they finally manage to liberate their people.

3. An ordinary person one day finds him/herself caught up in a life-and-death intrigue involving crime or espionage. Suddenly, ruthless killers are after something she/he is supposed to have but doesn't. Many chases, hidings, narrow escapes happen as the main character gets more and more involved. She/he helps the "good guys" even though it involves risk. In the end, she/he falls in love with one of the good guys, who helps to defeat the bad guys.

4. An ordinary vacation turns into a nightmare when terrorists (or extraterrestrial beings) take over the resort hotel in which the protagonist is staying. S/he must find ways to overcome the terrifying situation.

5. Twelve people are invited to be dinner guests at a huge unlived-in mansion on a rainy night. The electricity fails and the lights go out. When candles are found and lit, the group discovers that one of them has been murdered. The group is stranded at the mansion because all the roads to it are impassable. They must spend the night there. During the night, there is more murder and mayhem. You must find the murderer.

BEGIN LONG STORIES WITH FRAGMENTS

Most professional novelists have a very general skeleton in mind, but begin their book by writing fragments of it, rather than having the entire plot worked out in their minds. By writing these fragments, they are building a story, but often still don't know what the whole plot will eventually look like. Fragments could be descriptions of people, places and actions you see in your mind, conversations you imagine, letters you feel compelled to write, and so on.

You might do better to write your "book" in this way - as a collection of interesting vignettes - rather than try to follow a plot you have already decided on. The reason is that by writing fragments, you can be more creative. Another reason is that it is more fun, and it feels like less work, if you write vignettes or fragments, rather than sticking to a predetermined plot. In the end when you put your book together, you may decide not to use one or more of these fragments, or maybe you will use them all. (I'm sure, by the way, that your teacher will include them all in your 10,000 word requirement!)

Another consideration is that you may start out wanting to write a novel, but then as you write, you may decide on a collection of short stories instead. Allowing yourself this freedom will enhance your creativity as you write.

List here some possible "vignettes" you might tell and present as separate chapters in your book.

_____

_____

_____

_____

_____

OR BEGIN WITH SETTINGS AND CHARACTERS

If I couldn't think of good fragments to write, I would begin with the setting and characters. I would try to imagine the setting vividly in my mind: to see it, to hear the sounds there, to smell it, and to feel it. Within this setting, I would begin introducing my characters. I would use physical descriptions and start to describe the relationships among the characters. Then I would move quickly into the conflict, or the main reason I wanted to write the book. There are plenty of reasons for conflicts: territory, money, love, jealousy, good vs. evil, invasions, crimes, injustices, and so on. I would describe actions surrounding the conflict, but also write dialogues: arguments, promises of love, humorous exchanges; and monologues: messages, letters, memories, soliloquies, descriptions of dreams, and even speeches. Sometimes it is even necessary to write brief life stories of characters in order for your readers to understand what made them what they are today, or brought them into the circumstances of the story.

To start working on your book, choose one of the following: description of setting, character descriptions, character relationships, life stories, vignettes, dialogues (arguments, humorous exchanges, conversations, promises of love, etc.) or monologues (letters, speeches, recollections, diary entries, messages, soliloquies, dreams, memories), or even the conflict itself. Think about it for a while, and use your **observational** and **creative** abilities. Then start writing that part and do not stop to make any corrections. Do it like a free-write. And take as much time as you need. But **do not labor** over it. Write it as if you were trying to videotape something, capturing the best and the essence of it. When you finish, share it with a partner, but this time, only ask your partner to tell you what s/he **liked**. And for the rest of the book, do the same: find out what your reader liked.

The reason is that the most important thing for you to do now is to entertain your readers. **DO NOT BORE YOUR READERS**. This is a cardinal rule for writing. You can shock them, scare them, make them laugh, make them cry, make them remember or see something beautiful, make them think, make them feel guilty, righteous, uncomfortable or secure, or make them hate or love something. But don't make them yawn or not want to continue reading.

Most people enjoy a good story. Short stories may be about conflicts, joys, fights, romances, embarrassing moments, mysteries, funny incidents, tragedies, racist episodes, children's pranks or activities, and just about anything else. They are slices of life that can be read in a short time. Characters in short stories can be everyday ordinary people or mysterious or powerful people. But they give a whole story in a relatively short piece.

THE JOY OF SUSPENSE

If you choose to write a long story or a novel, you can sustain your readers' interest not only by the content, but by the way you structure your book. One of the great joys of reading, watching a movie, or just hearing a story told is the **suspense**, the wondering about what will happen next. It is no accident, therefore, that a writer plans to give the audience the excitement of suspense... of suspending them for a while in uncertainty and guessing while other parts of the story, character descriptions, monologues, or dialogues occur. I'm sure you've experienced suspense in your life: a kind of delightful uncertainty where you must try to figure out what will happen next.

To build this suspense into your book, you must structure it in such a way that your reader's knowledge builds gradually, but there are still many unanswered questions. Think of the book you are currently reading: how has the author built up suspense? What do you know?

What things are still unknown to you that you are anxious to find out? How has the author accomplished this? What did s/he tell you first, second, etc.? Now think about and discuss these questions, and why you still want to read on.

A fictional plot usually begins with a complication of some kind, a crisis, and an untangling of that crisis (in French, the denouement). Let's take a look at how mysteries, adventures, science fiction, and romances are written. All the while, be thinking which you'd most like to write.

WRITING A MYSTERY
(Partially adapted from *Teaching and Writing Popular Fiction*.)

Some of the most enjoyable reading is mystery reading. As we read mysteries, we try to discover secrets: who committed the crime, how it was committed, the motive, the concealment, and the unraveling. Mysteries are full of unexpected surprises and turns. The writer keeps us guessing until the very last. Mysteries keep us on the edge of our seats because generally they include fear, secrecy, violence, a victim, clues, darkness, chases, shootouts, captures, trials, convictions and other things that ordinary people are scared of. The criminals involved are unique. They do terrible things that we would never dream of doing.

Those who solve the crime are also unusual people. They take great risks, have unusual insight, have to survive by their wits, and have to figure out the truth from bits and pieces of seemingly unrelated evidence. They also have to notice things that escape the ordinary person. They have to be above suspicion, yet know about the evil workings of the human mind. They do not have to look heroic (tall, dark, handsome men; or beautiful women), but they do have to act heroically when necessary, and outwit their suspects.

HOW MYSTERIES ARE WRITTEN

Generally speaking, there is first a crime: a murder, a robbery, a kidnapping, an arson, or another serious crime. There are also various people: victims, detectives, policemen, eyewitnesses, character witnesses, suspects, and possibly gangsters or soliloquies. There are things like guns, fingerprints or pieces of hair or skin, knives, footprints, scribbled messages of victims, things left behind by the criminal, and other clues to the crime. Then there is the pursuit: surveillance, chases, shootouts, fights. This is followed by the capture or surrender: handcuffing, reading of legal rights, booking, arraignment, and incarceration. Then come the trial, witnesses, testimony, prosecution and defense, the verdict and sentencing.

Once the crime is committed, someone often tries to conceal it. The detective looks for clues and follows suspects to see if they give him any leads in solving the crime. He suddenly finds he is in danger. He either escapes or fights it out with the suspect and wins. This way he solves the mystery. Often there is a confession or a tacit understanding of the guilt of the suspect through his/her actions at the end.

Some mysteries begin when a corpse is found. Others begin when an innocent person is accused of a crime, or is an inadvertent witness to a crime. As the sleuth tries to solve the crime, with or without the help of a sidekick, s/he sees things that ordinary mortals miss. S/he knows that even when a case is air-tight, there is something amiss. Following intuition and hunches, s/he solves the mystery.

Witnesses or victims struggle through anonymous threats on their lives (mysterious phone calls, letters, shots through their windows). They come home to a wrecked apartment. They pour over mug shots in police records; they sit behind a one-way mirror and view lineups of suspects. Some shady witnesses attempt to blackmail the criminal instead of reporting him or her. Meanwhile the detective is interrogating everyone, studying clues, and taking notes (mental and/or physical) on the various pieces of the puzzle.

Often, a romance is woven into the story. The detective and an innocent witness being sought by the criminal fall in love. He protects her, but she must be brave and in so doing, helps to solve the crime. The detective is constantly vigilant and constantly asking questions...of himself and others. In the end, he solves the mystery, there is a trial, the criminal is convicted and sentenced, and if there is a romance, they get married.

Exercise 1

Take a few minutes and write below the skeleton of a mystery or a mystery/romance that you might write. This will help you decide if you would enjoy writing such a story or book.

Exercise 2

Now try to write a scary story. Think of something that will horrify your readers: a true horror story or an invented one. You could write about the scariest dream or experience you ever had. It could have been something you imagined as a child lying in bed in a dark room, or a real event which threatened your life. It could be about real world events or other-worldly. It could include bats, werewolves, ghosts, zombies, thieves or murderers in the night, stranglers lurking in hallways, falls into deep abysses or from high cliffs, monsters, poisonous or mind-altering potions, vampires, kidnappings, being chased by a murderous maniac or being lost in a scary place with strange sounds. It could take place in graveyards, underground tunnels, foreign countries, abandoned dungeons, dark basements or attics. Or you could write about a dream that was so bad that it woke you up. But try to capture those things that horrified you.

WRITING AN ADVENTURE (Partially adapted from *Teaching and Writing Popular Fiction*, by Karen M. Hubert)

If you like adventure movies - about wars, death-defying feats, ocean voyages, treks across wildernesses, espionage, science-fiction , people facing terrible odds, interplanetary or intergalactic conflicts and the like - you will probably enjoy reading and writing such stories.

Your adventure could be about a hunt for buried treasure, man against nature, a kidnapping, a race, a rescue, an escape, a battle, a competition, a chase, or an intrigue. Your protagonist could be trapped somewhere, taken prisoner, mistaken for the wrong person, abandoned in the wilderness, caught in a storm, being pursued by killers, captured by aliens or desperately trying to survive somewhere. Maybe s/he is trying to save the country from disaster, to find a kidnapped president, to help people survive a plane crash in the snowy mountains, or to prevent some terrible disaster.

There might be car chases, fights, torture, lack of food, sleep, water, darkness, fear, and loneliness. Your hero or heroine might wake up a different person, or only two inches tall. S/he might be trying to uncover the mysteries of the Bermuda triangle or the sinking of a great ocean liner. Perhaps in a foreign prison or an alien land, your hero/heroine might be trying to escape or outwit his captors.

An adventure story is one of a test of the protagonist's strength and wits against formidable odds and opponents, whether nature, people or superhuman beings. Your protagonist is probably looking for a person, a place or a thing. S/he has to kill or capture or rescue a person or people. As the protagonist pursues this goal, enemies put terrible obstacles in his way. The hero/heroine must overcome these obstacles. S/he must also be brave, strong, clever, resourceful and idealistic.

Your protagonist will be on a journey or a crusade to make right a wrong. He or she may explore, discover, or transform things. Your hero is also likeable and trustworthy, and never gives up. The action will leave your readers in suspense: there will be tests for your protagonist, and terrible odds to overcome. But in the end, despite setbacks, s/he will overcome any obstacle.

WRITING SCIENCE-FICTION (Partially adapted from *Teaching and Writing Popular Fiction*, by Karen M. Hubert)

If you enjoy science fiction stories or adventure/science fiction, you might enjoy writing one. Watch some science fiction movies and focus on **how** science fiction stories are developed.

In science fiction, the theme is usually deals with human reactions to radical changes in life as we know it on earth. These changes will probably include technological ones, and may well include sociological, psychological and philosophical ones as well. There also may be time warps, space warps, threats of destruction, robots, androids, alien forms of life, and lost worlds. There are usually advanced technologies, exploration and often colonization. And often there are new sociological and cultural situations as a result. The characters often encounter new faiths and religions, and sometimes changes in the psyche. The setting may be on earth or another planet, or in space between celestial bodies. The scenery, however, will be very different from our own surroundings, and the human characters will react to them.

Science fiction characters usually take intergalactic or interplanetary trips in spaceships that are propelled at great speeds. They are comfortable traveling throughout the cosmos. There is usually a male protagonist who is heroic and a born explorer and warrior. The female protagonist is beautiful and feminine, and very resourceful.

58

Like the male protagonist, she is strong and adventurous. The other characters serve to enhance the importance of the protagonists, and have much lesser roles and importance. But the opponents are very important, creating the tension and suspense in the story. They are the complete opposites of the protagonists.

The beginning chapters will tell the five W's, introduce the major characters, and describe the relationships among them. Then there will be a circumstance or event, a crisis, that will give rise to conflicts, complications, minor clashes and steadily rising action. There may be threats, challenges, then battles, intrigue, narrow escapes, and the use of every form of technology possible. The action will intensify and it will be hard to tell who will win. Then there will be a major climax with a crucial encounter. Here problems are finally resolved; mysteries are explained. Throughout the protagonists will have some victories but just as many setbacks, because struggle is the essence of science fiction. But in the end, s/he or they will prevail, and will have a new world or a new vision or dream.

WRITING A ROMANCE (Partially adapted from *Teaching and Writing Popular Fiction*, by Karen M. Hubert)

A romance is the story of a relationship and the feelings associated with it. It tells about how people meet, get to know one another, get close, separate, reunite, start again and deal with conflicts until love prevails and they remain together. Romances usually contain tests of the couple's love for one another: tests caused by jealousy, forced separations, and other obstacles. A romance may be combined with a mystery or an adventure story. It may even be combined with a comedy, but the is focus will be mainly on the relationship.

There may be a romantic setting, or one that is mundane. But there is often a loneliness in the protagonists, a sense of expectation, and a longing for love. The protagonists are good people who deserve to be loved. They may also be good-looking, but this is not required. The hero may be the strong, silent type, and the heroine demure and sincere. Or they may both be comedic. But both are trustworthy and likeable.

The story usually begins with their meeting, then their physical descriptions, then their getting to know each other through actions or through accounts of their pasts, then physical overtures toward each other, closeness and declarations of love. After this, their love is usually tested with obstacles, like temptations, rivals, jealousy, rumors, or conflicts over money, relatives, betrayal, or each other's pasts. There may be quarrels too. The suspense builds as the reader wonders if the romance will last. There may be fears, anger, sadness and yearning. But in the end, love prevails, there is exaltation and fulfillment. The hero usually proposes marriage to the heroine, and they live happily ever after.

Some romances build up within an adventure the couple is involved in: solving a murder mystery, espionage, a journey, a catastrophe, or a war, for example. Readers enjoy the combination of emotion and excitement in such stories. But even in these stories, the romance is just as important as the other part of the plot.

People in love have poignant dialogues, write to each other, write in their diaries, fantasize, and see beauty in each other. They are strongly attracted to each other, and often suffer when they are apart. The trick is to describe these feelings with dialogue and descriptive passages, while keeping the action moving. In addition to choosing romance as your genre, you have to think of the type of romance you will write about. Think about some romance movies that you have really enjoyed, and then consider planning to write stories of that nature.

CHAPTER SIX

DIALOGUES, MONOLOGUES, AND OTHER COMPOSING TECHNIQUES

WRITING DIALOGUES

Through conversations or dialogues with people, we come to know how they think, what they've done, their plans, their disappointments, their hopes, and their fears. People's words also reveal their priorities and their preoccupations. They can help to tell what's happening in a piece of fiction, relationships among characters, and conflicts. And for writers, dialogue writing is one of the most enjoyable, creative forms of writing.

To begin experimenting with dialogue writing, first write down a real dialogue that you heard between two other people. It doesn't have to be written word for word; it should just sound like a real conversation. Here's an example:

"Where did you get that gun?"
"None of your business."
"I demand to know. Where did you find that gun?"
"I didn't find it. I borrowed it."
"Whoever lent it to you is the murderer."
"What? But that's impossible!"

Now read it to your partner and ask him or her if it sounds like a real dialogue. Or you might want to write a dialogue **with** your partner, with each of you taking a role. Then discuss whether it sounds like a real dialogue. Once you've finished, go back and add any descriptions of **how** the lines should sound, and other necessary material, if just the dialogue alone doesn't do the trick. For example:

> *"Where did you get that gun?", she demanded angrily.*
> *He bluntly replied "None of your business", putting the*
> *gun into his pocket.*
> *"I demand to know", she said, shaking him bodily, her lips*
> *tightened and her eyes narrowed with anger, "Where did you get*
> *that gun?"*

Exercise 1

Now see if you and your partner can develop this dialogue into a short play with a complete plot. Try to write it with as little **talk** between yourselves as possible. That way, what you write will contain the meaning you both intended. Then when you're finished writing, discuss where you need to revise the lines of the play and revise it.

Exercise 2

Now write two pieces. First, write a dialogue that reveals the characters' inner selves and motives. Next, write a dialogue revealing a conflict. It could be between two leaders of warring nations, or two neighbors with a conflict. Make it realistic. For each of these, you could write collaboratively with a partner. Talk about the characters and the action before you write. But once you start writing, keep the talk between you and your partner to a minimum. Try to write at least one of the pieces on your own. After both, read, discuss, and revise them with your partner.

WRITING MONOLOGUES

Monologues, or one character talking (alone or to others) is another wonderful way to develop characters and plot. Some monologues are stream-of-consciousness types, whereas others are like little speeches directed to the reader or a group. They are also a way to reveal the thoughts of a character. And most important, they **sound** like the character; they are written in the character's way of talking and thinking. They are also typical of the character's personality.

Actually, you have already done a great deal of monologue writing by freewriting in your writing journals and writing in your double-entry journal entries. Monologue writing is also a way of thinking on paper. Your monologue writing reveals your feelings too: anger, impatience, self-confidence or lack thereof, frustration, exhilaration, confusion, etc.

Well, in fiction writing, you may use monologue writing in many ways: a confession, a speech made by a character defending him/herself, a diary entry, a person talking to herself or himself, a self-analysis, a request for help or understanding, talking through a problem to try to resolve it, a self-portrait, feelings of not belonging or of inadequacy, a first-hand account of an event, a dream, or even a whole or most of a novel or play told in first person.

To write convincing monologues for characters, you must really feel sympathetic toward them, and get inside their heads. It's hard to write convincingly if you do not do this.

Exercise 3

Try doing some freewriting to get some ideas for monologue writing. Focus on your own thoughts first. First freewrite for ten minutes describing what is going on in your own mind right now: thoughts, scenes, apprehensions, plans, and so on. Then think about how one of your characters in your book, or yourself in your autobiography, can reveal so much about him or herself through this type of stream-of-consciousness writing.

Exercise 4

Another technique is to talk to yourself. Do a ten minute freewrite talking to yourself on paper: giving yourself advice, reminding yourself to do something, getting angry at yourself, patting yourself on the back, complaining, or whatever you ordinarily do when you talk to yourself. (Even if you don't talk to yourself out loud, most of us talk to ourselves in our minds.) Just write the talk that's going through your mind.

Another way to develop monologue is to have a conversation **with yourself**... an actual dialogue you have with yourself. You could have two sides of your personality talk to yourself: the wise side to the foolish side, the saver to the spender, the romantic to the practical, and so on.

Other ideas for monologues are to make lists, write down observations, examine things and describe them, do a fictional diary (things you might do/have done, felt, worried about). Write memoirs: about disasters, about what the future will hold, etc. Tell why you want to go on living your life; tell of the man/woman of your dreams. Make a speech on your own behalf, or make your presidential inauguration speech, etc.

CHAPTER SEVEN

WRITING DESCRIPTIONS

DESCRIBING PEOPLE

In addition to telling a good story, or actually as part of telling a good story, you need to give your readers the ability to **see** your characters as you do. To describe a person, you need as many details as possible: age, size, shape, color (hair, skin, clothing), textures, voice, walk, posture, odor, facial expressions, gestures, and unique physical characteristics (moles, scars, tumors, eye patches, nervous twitches, obesity, frailty), and other details like neatness, cleanliness, peculiarity of dress, or distinguishing details of dress.

In describing people, it is good to appeal to your readers' senses: sight, smell, touch, hearing, and even taste. Thus use terms that are as **vivid** as possible.

Exercise 1

Think of a person you can **see** vividly in your mind. Close your eyes if you have to and really look at that person. Pick out the things about him or her that stand out the most in your mind. Then write a **physical** description of that person, including bodily details, and details about clothing, posture, and other physical characteristics.

When you have finished, close your eyes again and **see** that person. Look for important distinguishing details that you have missed...ones that you would definitely include if you were drawing a picture of that person. Now add these to your written description. **(Time to write)**

You will probably also want to describe the person's way of speaking and otherwise interacting with people. This will lead to further description of the person's apparent emotional or psychological state, education, and even their character. Some adjectives you might find useful are: withdrawn, pensive, shy, soft-spoken, guarded, inebriated, fearful, suspicious, loud, joyful, dramatic, bubbly, confident, self-conscious, shaken, steady, forceful, weak, sly, straightforward, cocky, guileless, self-effacing, down-to-earth, unassuming, elusive, talkative, curt, abrupt, friendly, spontaneous, direct, demure, outspoken.

In short, try to describe what that person is like: mood, character, speech, disposition, behaviors, values and other characteristics. Give enough details to help the reader to get a good idea of the kind of person you are describing. You might want to make a list of adjectives first; then continue writing your character description.

Exercise 2

Write a few pieces or paragraphs on three or four of the following topics. Describe (i.e. give a physical description of):

    a.   a person with a bad cold or flu.
    b.   a newborn baby.
    c.   a police officer or a military person.
    d.   yourself.
    e.   a famous political or military leader.
    f.   a person you love.

g.   your ideal marriage partner.

h.   a favorite teacher.

i.   a crime suspect as the police might describe him or her.

j.   a character from your neighborhood.

k.   a serial murderer.

l.   a crazy person.

m.   an alcoholic, a drug addict, or a derelict.

n.   an exaggeration of a person.

o.   a sickly, dying or dead person.

p.   a person who is angry, depressed, or otherwise upset.

q.   a scary person.

r.   a person in a play, movie, opera, or T.V. program.

s.   a person you admire from a distance and would like to know.

t.   a child.

u.   a character in the novel you plan to write.

Read each piece you have written to your writing group, and get feedback on it. Then revise it to make it as interesting and vivid as possible.

DESCRIBING PLACES

Just as in describing a person, to describe a place well you must be a **good observer**. You must not only see all the details of a place, but be able to pick out the ones that will most vividly let your readers **see** it as you do. Your readers should not only **see** the place vividly, but should **feel** it as you do or as you wish them to. Thus, you may add **actions** to your description of a place: who's doing what, what's happening, where people are located, what people are saying, and so on.

And as in describing people, you want to appeal to the senses: sights, smells, textures, noises, and ambience. Try to capture these with descriptive words, and with language that specifies size, shapes, location, activity level, and the combination of all of these as setting.

Exercise 3

To practice describing places, start with where you are right now: your classroom. Or perhaps your class might go out and visit another place on campus: the library, the cafeteria, the center of the campus, or some other spot. Study the spot and with a partner, write as complete a description of it as possible...enough so that an artist might be able to sketch it from your description. Once you and your partner have written the physical description, try to write a description of the atmosphere or ambience of the place. Remember, you want your reader to feel like he or she is there. Before and while you and your partner are writing, discuss details and actions. Then try to write them as precisely and evocatively as possible, capturing the ambience of the place as well as a pretty exact description of it.

Exercise 4

A good exercise for writing place descriptions is to write about a place you have very strong feelings about: you might hate it, love it, fear it, be disgusted by it, or have fond memories of it. Write a piece describing it physically, with action details that would give a sense of its emotional meaning to your readers as well. It could be your home, a subway, a park, a cemetery, a room, a church, an office, a business place, a factory, a battlefield, a government office, a restaurant, an athletic facility, a street, city or town, a beach, and so on. Read this piece to your partner and get his/her feedback. Revise it until you think it paints the place well and evokes in your readers the feelings it evokes in you.

WHERE AM I?

Another good exercise to build your descriptive vocabulary is to play the game, "I'm thinking of a place" and let your classmates listen to your description and guess where it is. The place should not be an easy one to guess, but should allow the listeners to have fun and enjoy the competition as they strive to be the winner, or the one who guesses the place. Let me give you a couple of examples.

I'm thinking of a place that is stark white. It is round and there is nothing else to see except the white contours surrounding me. It is all the same, whether I look up, down, to the right or to the left. And it is a place where I can only stay for a few minutes, lest I die of suffocation. I can tell if the sun is shining or if there is artificial light outside of this place. The whiteness of it becomes even brighter. But if it is dark out, this place is penetrated by darkness, and the whiteness of it is barely discernible in the darkness. It's a bit difficult to stand in this place because it is completely round. And one more thing, to fit into it, I must temporarily shrink to the size of a bumble bee or a lady bug. A butterfly or a mouse would be too big. If I try to run inside of this place, it will move round and round and round. Where am I?

I'm thinking of a place where there is never any sunlight. Many people come and go from there every day. Sometimes the crowds are so big that you can barely move, but must go with the flow of other bodies. There are pungent smells of filth there: dirt, rotten garbage, smoke from cigarettes, cigars, marijuana and engine exhausts, odors from loiterers who haven't bathed in a long time, and the grit and grime of years of neglect. The place is relatively barren, with a few benches, pillars, and walls that have absorbed too many coats of dingy paint. There are discarded newspapers and other refuse scattered here and there, and there is graffiti everywhere. Some of it is obscene; the rest is political, personal or simply absurd.

Art it is not. The place is usually pretty quiet, filled with strangers who do not talk to or even look at each other. Then in the distance one can hear the thundering approach of wheels and a monotonous pre-recorded announcement. Where am I?

(Answers: #1, Inside a ping-pong ball; #2, NYC subway station

Exercise 5

Write three pieces, choosing from the following topics. Then share them with your group and revise them.

a. The report of the scene of a crime or accident.
b. A teenager's bedroom.
c. An imaginary planet.
d. Planet earth from the viewpoint of an extraterrestrial being.
e. The inside of a computer, radio, T.V., car engine, etc.
f. A mother's womb from the viewpoint of her unborn child.
g. A prison cell.
h. A supermarket, a toy store, or a fresh air market.
i. A morgue or a funeral home.
j. A hospital operating room.
k. A neighborhood or a section of a city.
l. A museum or a church.
m. A zoo or a farm.
n. A dream house or a favorite hiding place.
o. An abandoned building or a garbage dump.
p. Ancient ruins or modern cities.
q. The world from the top of a skyscraper or a jet plane.
r. What you see as you travel through a place.
s. Your first impression of the United States or of New York City.
t. A tour through a place.
u. The evening sky or the earth at dawn.

DESCRIBING ACTIONS

If you described a place on campus, you probably included actions like, "gentle breezes through the trees," "students hurrying to and fro," "students leisurely strolling and chatting excitedly with friends," "bright banners flapping from upper floor windows," "fallen leaves being shuffled here and there by the wind," "a game of touch football blocking traffic," "a few student activists passing out pamphlets," and other descriptions of actions. You might also have included feelings: "a joyful sight", "...making me laugh", and so on. As with people and places, you must describe actions so that your readers may **see** them as you do. To describe actions you must include the 5 W's: **WHO, WHAT, WHEN, WHERE**, and **WHY**.

Exercise 6

To start describing actions, first try to describe the actions involved in doing one of the following actions:

      a.   getting into a car, starting it up, and driving away
      b.   smoking a cigarette
      c.   preparing a meal

Exercise 7

Next, write directions for someone on how to do one of these:

      a.   How to drive in a busy city.
      b.   How to type without looking at the keyboard.
      c.   How to play soccer, basketball, football, etc.
      d.   How to meet and marry the person of your dreams.
      e.   How to rob a bank, hijack a plane, or escape from prison.

WHY IS ACTION SO IMPORTANT?

The heart of a story is the action, and the key to writing effectively about action is **observation**. You must be a keen observer of things you really see or things you imagine if you are writing creatively. Make real pictures in your mind of the characters, scenes and actions, and then describe the actions as they happen. Try to see them in **slow motion** if necessary, in order to capture the details that will make the reader see the actions as you see them. And remember to add other details of **description, talk or mental state** that complete the description of the action. To describe actions, we not only answer the five "W" questions, but we also add enough **descriptive detail** for the reader to **see** the action as we see it.

Exercise 8

Think of some action you have observed and are familiar with. For example, a bank robbery, a surgical operation, or an accident you witnessed, a skating performance, a person getting ready for a big date, someone making something, a child at play, a baby feeding herself, a sporting event, a fight, a brush with danger, a terrorist takeover of an airplane, a scene at a beach or park, a scene of a person receiving bad or good news, a car chase, a dinner table scene, a shy person trying to make a friend, a crazy person talking to her/himself, a funny mishap, or a mysterious-looking person and what you observed him/her do.

Now pretend you are a newspaper writer and report on one of the them. Describe it and then speculate on its impact, importance, the human element, or other aspects of interest.

Now read your piece to your group and revise it, but do it as if you were preparing to publish it in a real newspaper or a magazine.

CHAPTER EIGHT

NOTICING AUTHORS' TECHNIQUES

Now that you have been reading your novel for a while, writing double-entry journal notes, and discussing the novel in class with your reading group, you are probably also beginning to notice **how** writers write in English. Try to notice at least one of those techniques every day that you read, and note it in your journal to mention to your group members. Look for the following techniques:

character descriptions
descriptions of people, places, things
action descriptions
dialogues and monologues
chapter beginnings and endings
unfinished episodes

Notice how the author uses description, talk and action to reveal what the characters are like, especially contrasts and conflicts between them, and their inner motives and feelings. Here are some contrasts that an author might develop:

honest vs. dishonest
straightforward vs. elusive
educated vs. uneducated
antagonistic vs. conciliatory
scheming vs. guileless

brave vs. cowardly
weak vs. strong
trusting vs. suspicious
verbose vs. laconic
truthful vs. mendacious

Remember, people often reveal their characters as they speak. Things like cynicism, cowardice, bravery, honesty, and other characteristics can surface through a person's words as well as her/his actions.

Also notice how the adjectives used describe the person physically and morally. And of course, notice how their actions match their characters.

Exercise 1

Now go through the pages of the book you are currently working on - only the pages you have read so far - and find some examples of **monologue**. Read these to your reading group and discuss the "voice" of the person whose monologue it is: i.e. discuss how his/her personality, attitudes, hidden and overt agendas, etc. come through in the monologue.

Exercise 2

Next, try to find some **dialogue** revealing the voices and characters of two or more people. Discuss how the author weaves together action and character development.

Exercise 3

Now look for some straight **description**. It might be of the character's physical appearance, character, mental state, motives, or emotional state. Discuss how the author wrote this description with your peers.

Exercise 4

In these monologues, dialogues and descriptions, how does the author develop contrasts between and among characters? Discuss these contrasts with your peers.

As you read your books, notice how authors begin scenes, how they end them, where they leave you guessing, and generally how they manipulate you into wanting to keep reading the book. These are techniques that make a piece of writing interesting. Since you have probably done a good deal of reading, you may already know or recognize or perhaps even use some of these techniques in your own writing.

Exercise 5

Go through the pieces you have written so far. Write below some of your best opening sentences. Then the class will share them.

_____
_____
_____
_____
_____
_____
_____
_____
_____
_____
_____
_____
_____

Exercise 6

Look again at the book you are currently reading and try to find some examples of how the author begins scenes or chapters. Notice how the author may leave unanswered questions, go back to the past, go forward, etc. List some of them below, then read and discuss them with your reading group.

Now study how the author ends scenes and chapters. You will probably be able to write in pretty concrete terms the techniques the author is using. List them below as well. Then try to find some examples of how an author leaves readers guessing and wanting to find out what happens next. Again, use the book you are currently reading or one you have recently finished reading. Try to figure out **why** the author is structuring the plot in this way.

Beginnings

_____
_____
_____
_____

Endings

_____
_____
_____
_____

Finally, discuss with your peers the **actions** so far in the book. Re-read some action parts and discuss these. How does the author relate them? What does the author include? What can you see or imagine by reading them? How do they further the plot?

CHAPTER NINE

REVISING

WHAT IS REVISION?

To revise means to look again at what you've written, and to improve it by making additions or deletions, by moving text, by using a more precise word, or by rewording or combining sentences for a smoother flow of ideas.

WHY REVISE?

It has been said by many that the real work of writing begins once the first draft is finished. Almost no one writes a perfect piece the first time around. That's why you have been asked to read aloud all of your 10,000 word project pieces to a partner or a group, get feedback from them, and to revise based on that feedback before giving the piece to your teacher for feedback, after which you might revise again. Revising with others' help eventually helps you to revise on your own.

RESPONDING TO WRITING

What kinds of responses can help someone reading a piece for feedback? Constructive ones, not destructive ones. Ones that indicate the strong parts of the piece, for example. You could say what you liked best, what you remembered, what you learned, or how you felt listening to the piece.

Your reactions can begin with words like, "I noticed...", "For me,..." "I think...", "I like...", "I don't understand...", "I'm confused about...", "This reminds me of...", "Why did...? and so on.

The point of collaborating with peers is not to criticize each other, but to **help** each other. Once you write a rough draft, you need to read it to someone else to find out what it says to them. That way, you'll know if/what they like about it, how/if their expectations have been met, and what needs to be added, deleted, moved or improved. You'll also know if the piece is fluent. Following are the criteria for fluency. **A fluent piece is complete, logical, devoid of gaps or unnecessary material, comprehensible and engaging to read**.

Remember, too, that the writing focus in this book is on **composing,** rather than editing. So focus on composing issues when you work with a partner: writing, talking, sharing, thinking, anticipating audience needs, revising, rewriting. Don't worry for now about spelling, mechanics, sentence boundaries or word endings. You'll do that once you are satisfied with the contents of your pieces. But as I've said previously, be assured that these things will improve the more you write.

Make sure you tell your partner honestly what you think of a piece. Give the good news first - what you liked, what you learned, why you wanted to read on. Then tell the author where the rough spots are. Here are some ways to respond to a piece of writing:
1. What I liked the most about this piece is:
2. I would really like to hear more about:
3. What sounds best in the piece is:
4. What I find most memorable is:
5. My question(s) is/are:
6. The focus of this piece seems to be:
7. If this were my paper, I would:
8. I don't quite understand:

HELPING YOUR PARTNERS TO REVISE

As a writing partner or group member reads the piece aloud to you, try to look at it and follow along. Stop him or her to ask questions if you are confused, to indicate repetitions or gaps, to indicate parts you like, or to indicate that he or she has read something that isn't there or vice versa (not read something that is there). This will help the writer of the piece to do the most important thing: read and revise his or her own pieces, a most difficult thing for a writer to do.

When a member of your group is finished reading the piece to you, respond with non-judgmental, helpful statements like: **what you liked about the piece; if/why you want to read on; what you learned from reading it; where you think more information is needed; part(s) that may have confused you.**

REVISING ALONE

Both during and after reading a piece to your group, the writer should be revising as necessary.

Revising includes:
> **making changes,**
> **additions,**
> **deletions,**
> **corrections,**
> **insertions**, or
> **moving pieces of the text**.

Look at the revised piece on the following page. Notice that the author doesn't erase the original text, but simply puts a line through it. This is in case she or he decides later that the original was the best choice. Also notice how the writer writes on every other line, making it easier to revise.

EVEN WEAKLINGS CAN STOP SMOKING

One reason you should stop smoking is that it might kill you. Smoking is ~~not~~ a ^dangerous ~~healthy~~ practice. (*Insert statistics on lung disease for active and passive smokers.*) It might kill your family members, too.^ It is a waste of money. Cigarettes are ^very expensive these days. *and health care for lung disease is prohibitive* But smokers have a terrible time giving up smoking. They say that it is ten times harder than going on a diet. And anyone who has gone on a diet knows that dieting is extremely hard. And ~~like~~ *with* dieting, once you give up smoking, it is hard to maintain that abstinence. ~~I heard once that~~ Ninety-five percent of dieters regain all the weight they lose. And ~~I read somewhere that~~ in the case of alcoholics, only five percent of those who join Alcoholics Anonymous stay with the program; the others resume drinking. ~~Then I have also heard that~~ Alcoholics say that giving up smoking is harder than giving up drinking. Well, all I know is that I smoked two packs a day for many years. Then I got pneumonia and had to stop *smoking or lose a lung.* After about two weeks, I never wanted a cigarette again. And I'm a certified weakling: I can't diet, I don't exercise, and I am basically lazy. If I can give it up, anyone can. All it takes is a good old healthy fear of dying.

IMPORTANT TIP ON WRITING THAT IS TO BE REVISED

In order to save yourself a lot of time, **write on one side of the page only, and on every other line**. That way, you can easily made insertions, deletions, and other changes. And you can cut and move parts of the text too, or just cut and eliminate them, pasting the rest of the piece together.

REVIEW

Remember to be positive and respectful as you give the kinds of responses your partners need to make their writing better, including the following:

1. Knowing what you liked about the piece and why you wanted to read on.

2. Knowing the confusing parts.

3. Knowing where gaps or superfluous material in the piece are.

4. Getting advice on how to make the piece more complete, more interesting, or more readable.

5. Knowing if the beginnings and endings are effective.

CHAPTER TEN

EDITING

DIFFERENCES BETWEEN COMPOSING & EDITING

Writers must compose, revise and edit their pieces, all different processes. Composing or writing well means writing pieces that people like to read because they are either interesting, thought-provoking, shocking, informative, entertaining, or touch the emotions. It does not mean writing correctly. Editing is correcting. And composing is far more important than editing. Too many students think that writing means producing something that teachers will find acceptable because it is written a certain way and has no errors. So they strive to avoid errors as they write, and to write in ways to please a teacher. Unfortunately, such pieces are usually hard to write and can be very dull and often confusing to read.

Writers have to realize that there are three jobs to do when writing. The first two are the most important: to compose pieces that are logical and engaging to read, and to revise them to make them as clear as possible. The third job is to edit them for errors. But when people are novices at writing and try to do all three simultaneously, they often do none of them well. That's why in this book, we have been focusing on composing rather than editing. If you do the writing suggested here **and** work with partners and alone to **revise** your pieces until they are really good, then you will have accomplished the most difficult and most important parts of writing: composing and revising. I advise you not to worry about editing until your pieces are written well enough to be published. Then, to eliminate the largest amount of errors, I suggest you do selective editing.

SELECTIVE EDITING

It is very hard to find and correct all of your errors in writing. But to get the largest number possible, it is good to edit for the kinds of errors you make the most. For example, if you have 42 errors on a piece - 20 verb errors, 14 punctuation errors, 1 spelling error, 2 preposition errors, 1 word form error, 3 article errors, and 1 capitalization error - probably the areas you need to concentrate on the most are verbs and punctuation. If you can eliminate those two types of errors, you only have 8, instead of 42, errors.

Now take a piece that has been corrected for errors. Categorize the errors as needed (see example below), and then count the number of those types of mistakes, putting the number under each category.

Verbs	Punct.	Pron.	Spell.	Art.	Wd. Forms	Preps.
20	14	1	1	2	1	1

Choose the one or two categories with the most errors to work on. Write these on a sheet of paper. Then further categorize your errors as "careless" or "real" (example below).

VERBS		PUNCTUATION	
Careless errors	Real errors	Careless errors	Real errors

Careless errors are the ones you can correct without help; real errors are the ones which you need help in correcting. If most of your errors are careless ones, as is usually the case, you will be able to find most of them in one or two categories, and thus correct most of your errors. If most of them are real errors, you will need help to understand the rules that apply.

Now take two other pieces that have been corrected, and categorize your errors as to type, and whether they are careless or real. Then correct them.

Having gone over three pieces, you should now be able to describe and find two or three types of your most frequently occurring errors. So now take 2 or 3 pieces that have not been corrected, and edit just for those types of errors. List below the two most frequent types, and do a count of them on your papers, listing the amounts below the categories, as well as the specific mistakes you made.

Careless	Real	:	Careless	Real

EDITING FOR PUNCTUATION ERRORS

One of the most common, and most serious mistakes in writing is to forget to put periods at the end of sentences. A good way to find and correct these errors is to read your pieces from the end to the beginning. That is, put your two index fingers on the last two periods of your written piece. Then read what's between those two periods. If it is a phrase like, ". For the rest of my life.", you will know that it is not a sentence, but only part of it, or a fragment. If there are many lines, there may be many sentences running together; these are called run-on sentences. So you must try to find the places where the narrative actually stops, and put periods there. If you keep going from the last sentence to the first, you are more likely to find and correct fragments and run-on sentences. These rules may also help:

PERIODS are necessary to mark sentence endings. Other marks that we use frequently are commas, semicolons, colons, question marks and exclamation marks. The two latter are easy to use. But you might have to refer to the following rules for the others:

COMMAS: separate items in a series and multiple adjectives; set off introductory phrases and clauses, and non-essential words, phrases and clauses.

COLONS: precede lists; emphasize points; separate related sentences when the second explains the first;and introduce quotations.

SEMICOLONS: separate independent clauses that are closely related and word groups already divided by commas

On the next page, edit for fragments and run-on sentences by using the technique described above: i.e. reading (from the end back) what's between periods to see if they are complete sentences.

Editing Practice: Run-ons and Fragments

Her hair was long, thick and black, her face was beautiful, she looked like a young movie star, she was twenty seven when I was born. I was the second. Of eight children. And she took care of all of us. Which wasn't easy. Sometimes my brothers would be wrestling on the floor and practically killing each other, sometimes someone would have a bloody nose. Or a bleeding facial gash. And there would be crying and shouting, "He did it" "No I didn't, you big brat, you did it." She wouldn't get angry or yell, she'd just try to separate them, patch up cuts, or tend to bruises, she didn't panic.

But when my father came home, if my mother happened to mention the trouble.. He'd go crazy. "Why do you have to give your mother such a hard time?" He would yell. "You know you're forbidden to fight in this house. Whether I'm here or not. That's the rule. For everyone in the house. Including all of you." And she'd say. "Dear, don't fuss, they'll behave better from now on, they promised me." "Now. Everyone wash your hands, let's all eat dinner, it's getting cold." Then he would calm down. After we all had assembled at the table. My father would say grace, and my mother would smile. And wink at us. Because by then, my father and my brothers had forgotten the fight. And were busy eating.

She used to wink at us a lot. Especially when she was giving us secret permission. To do something that our father would not allow. It was usually something like staying out later than we should have, she would give us permission but swear us to secrecy, we would have to plan what time we would sneak in. At that time. She would leave a door unlocked so that we could slip in unnoticed. Unless by chance Dad woke up or suddenly appeared where we weren't expecting him. But even so. He always forgave her after getting mad, he couldn't stay mad at her for long.

EDITING FOR VERB ERRORS

You have likely had a lot of instruction on the proper use of verbs. You should remember the forms to use. One of the most important things to remember in editing is to use the right tenses.

PRESENT TENSE is used for generalities, pronouncements and habits.

> e.g. I/you/we/they *KNOW/DON'T KNOW*;
> he/she/it *KNOWS/DOESN'T KNOW*

> e.g. We *don't like* it. I *quit*. He *doesn't talk* a lot.

PRESENT CONTINUOUS TENSE is used for present actions and future plans.

> e.g. I *AM/AM NOT EATING*; he/she/it *IS/ISN'T* or *'S NOT eating*; you/we/they *ARE/AREN'T EATING*

> e.g. It*'s raining*. We*'re getting married* in July.

PRESENT PERFECT TENSE is for actions that started in the past and continue; ones that have just occurred; questions with indefinite past time.

> e.g. I/you/we/they *HAVE/HAVEN'T WORKED*;
> he/she/it *HAS/HASN'T WORKED*

> e.g. We*'ve* always *lived* here. John *has arrived*. *Has* it *started*?

Some past participles do not end in -ed. Consult the following list.

Irregular Past Participles (do not end in -ed)

be - been

beat - beaten

become - became

begin - begun

bend - bent

bet - bet

bite - bitten

bleed - bled

break - broken

bring - brought

build - built

buy - bought

catch - caught

choose - chosen

come - come

cost - cost

cut - cut

deal - dealt

dig - dug

do - done

draw - drawn

drive - driven

eat - eaten

fall - fallen

feed - fed

feel - felt

fight - fought

find - found

fly - flown

lend - lent

let - let

lie - lied

lie - lain

light - lit

lose - lost

make - made

mean - meant

meet - met

pay - paid

put - put

quit - quit

read - read

ride - ridden

ring - rung

rise - risen

run - run

say - said

see - seen

sell - sold

send - sent

set - set

shake - shaken

shoot - shot

show - shown

shut - shut

sing - sung

sit - sat

sleep - slept

fit - fit
flee - fled
forget - forgotten
forgive - forgiven
freeze - frozen
get - gotten
give - given
go - gone
grow - grown
hang - hung
hear - heard
hide - hidden
hit - hit
hold - held
hurt - hurt
keep - kept
know - known
lay - laid
lead - led
leave - left

speak - spoken
spend - spent
spread - spread
stand - stood
steal - stolen
strike - stricken
sweep - swept
take - taken
teach - taught
tear - torn
tell - told
think - thought
throw - thrown
understand - understood
wear - worn
win - won
wind - wound
withdraw - withdrawn
wring - wrung
write - written

(This is not an exhaustive list.)

PRESENT PERFECT CONTINUOUS TENSE is used for recent sustained time/duration.

e.g. I/you/we/they *HAVE/HAVEN'T BEEN WAITING*;
he/she/it *HAS/HASN'T BEEN WAITING*

e.g. I*'ve been waiting* for an hour. It*'s been raining* all day.

PAST TENSE is used for completed actions, past generalities, and after wishes.

e.g.   I/you/we/they/he/she/it *WORKED/DIDN'T WORK* (N.B. See irregulars, next page.)

e.g. He *arrived* late. We *didn't know* her. I wish I *had 3*   wishes.

Some Past Tense Irregulars (do not end in -ed)

be - was/were	hang - hung	sell - sold
beat - beat	have - had	send - sent
become - became	hear - heard	set - set
begin - began	hide - hid	shake - shook
bet - bet	hit - hit	shine - shone
bite - bit	hold - held	shoot - shot
bleed - bled	hurt - hurt	shut - shut
blow - blew	keep - kept	sing - sang
break - broke	know - knew	sink - sank
catch - caught	lay - laid	sit - sat
bring - brought	lead - led	sleep - slept
build - built	leave - left	slide - slid
choose - chose	lend - lent	speak - spoke
come - came	let - let	spend - spent
cost - cost	lie - lied	spread - spread
do - did	lie - lay	stand - stood
draw - drew	light - lit	steal - stole
drink - drank	lose - lost	strike - struck
drive - drove	make - made	swear - swore
eat - ate	mean - meant	take - took
fall - fell	meet - met	teach - taught
feed - fed	pay - paid	tear - tore
feel - felt	put - put	tell - told

fight - fought	quit - quit	think - thought
find - found	read - read	throw - threw
forget - forgot	ride - rode	understand -
forgive - forgave	ring - rang	understood
freeze - froze	rise - rose	wake - woke
get - got	run - ran	wear - wore
give - gave	say - said	weep - wept
go - went	see - saw	wind - wound
grow - grew	seek - sought	write - wrote

PAST CONTINUOUS TENSE is used for an activity in progress in the past;

    e.g. I/he/she/it *WAS/WASN'T WAITING*;
        you/we/they *WERE/WEREN'T WAITING*

    e.g. *I was sleeping* when you called.

PAST PERFECT TENSE is used for past actions completed prior to other past actions;

    e.g. I/you/he/she/it/we/they *HAD/HADN'T WORKED*
        (Consult list of irregular past participles)

    e.g. By the time you called, I *had* already *left*.

PAST PERFECT CONTINUOUS TENSE is used for past continuous actions interrupted by another past action;

    e.g. I/you/she/it/he/we/they *HAD/HADN'T BEEN WORKING*

    e.g. By the time you called, I *had been working* for seven hours.

FUTURE TENSE is used for the future and for refusals, and polite requests;

 e.g. I/you/he/she/it/we/they *WILL/WON'T LEAVE*

 e.g. You *will be* 25 soon. I *won't do* it. *Will* you *help* me?

FUTURE CONTINUOUS TENSE is used for future events occurring at a certain time;

 e.g. I/you/she/he/it/we/they *WILL/WON'T BE GOING*

 e.g. It *will be snowing* this time next month.

FUTURE PERFECT TENSE is used for actions that will be completed in the future;

 e.g. I/you/she/he/it/we/they *WILL/WON'T HAVE ARRIVED*
  (See irregular past participles)

 e.g. By the year 2,000, I *will have worked* for 30 years.

MODALS indicate meaning, rather than time.
should/ought to/have to/must - indicate obligation or likelihood
can/could/may/might - indicate ability, possibility or permission
will/would - indicate intention, promise, refusal (with no)

N.B. Use modals with the perfect "have" and the past participle to put them in past tense. But with "must", the meaning changes in the past: "must have" means "probably". Also, be careful to spell the contracted forms correctly. People say "should of", "could of", and "must of" for the abbreviated "should've", "could've", "must've".
But don't spell them they way they're said.

IF/RESULT SENTENCES are constructed as follows:
For the future: If I see him, I will invite him. (present-future)
For the present: If I saw him, I would invite him. (past-conditional)
For the past: If I had seen him, I would have invited him.
                            (past perfect-conditional perfect)

EDITING FOR SUITABLE PARAGRAPHING

After you have written a piece, go back and see if your paragraphs are as accurate as you'd like them to be. What's most important about paragraphs is that they seem to be right in the **context** in which they appear. That is to say, they should go well with the paragraphs preceding and following them.

As you know, a paragraph is supposed to group together related sentences. When people read these units, or groups of sentences, they can remember what they're reading because of this grouping. Paragraphs also say and do something.   So a good way to check your paragraphs is to answer these questions for each one: "What does the paragraph say?" and" What does the paragraph do?" You should be able to briefly summarize what it says. If you cannot, perhaps it says too much and should be divided into two or more paragraphs. Then answer what it does. Things that a paragraph can do include the following: explain, illustrate, restate, introduce, give proof, restate important things, conclude, and so on.

Once you do this for each paragraph, you'll have an outline of the pieces in your book. Go over this outline to make sure that the pieces and the chapters of your book flow as you want them to, one to another, and to find out if you have any unnecessary parts or gaps. Then revise as needed.
(Adapted from *The Right Handbook*, by Belanoff et al. in 1986, Boynton-Cook Publishers, Inc., Portsmouth, New Hampshire.)

OTHER ISSUES OF MECHANICS

CAPITALIZING: Capitalize the first word in every sentence, proper names of people, countries, towns, states, oceans, rivers, buildings; streets, roads, boulevards, highways, and anything else with a proper name); the names of the months, the days, and the planets; titles preceding names; and abbreviations of titles (e.g. Dr., Ms., Mr., Mrs., Prof.).

UNDERLINING: Underline titles of books, magazines and newspapers.

USING QUOTATION MARKS: Use quotation marks before and after direct quotations, and for titles of plays, songs, paintings, poems, short stories, articles, essays and chapters in books.

EDITING FOR SPELLING ERRORS

If you have spelling errors, you must list them in a special section of your course notebook, study them, and test yourself on them until you know them. Ask a friend or relative to hear you, but study them. There is no other way to learn them. The following tips and rules may help, too.

Check your dictionary; or for even faster results, ask your teacher. If you work on a computer, use the spell checker. And as you read your books, try to photograph in your memory the spelling of new words, or say their spelling to yourself a few times without looking at the word. Read over the rules that follow, and consult them when necessary. But otherwise, don't worry about spelling for the time being. Worry about writing interesting stories!

RULES

1. "I" before "e", except after "c", and in some words that have the long "a" sound. For example: believe, retrieve, niece

    Exceptions: conceive, receive, ceiling,
                       neighbor, weigh, vein, deign, leisure, neither
                       science, either, height, seize, foreign, conscience

2. For one-syllable verbs ending in a vowel and a consonant, you m u s t double the final consonant before adding -ed or -ing.

    hop   hopped   hopping
    tip   tipped   tipping
    rot   rotted   rotting
    N.B. In such words, the vowel is "short".

3. For verbs ending in a consonant and "e", you do not double the f i n a l consonant, and you drop the "e", before adding -ed or -ing.

    hope   hoped   hoping
    advise advised   advising
    erode eroded   eroding

    N.B. In the syllables at the end of such verbs, the vowel is "long" (i.e. like the alphabet sound).

4. For verbs ending in a consonant and "y", you form the past by dropping the "y" and adding "ied".

cry/cried   rely/relied

hurry/hurried   carry/carried

5. For verbs ending in a vowel and "y", add "ed"

    play/played   toy/toyed

6. For two-syllable verbs that stress the second syllable and end in a vowel and consonant, double the final consonant before -ed and -ing.

defer	deferred	deferring
extol	extolled	extolling
expel	expelled	expelling

If the same kind of verb has the accent on the first syllable, just add -ed or -ing.

exit	exited	exiting
cancel	canceled	canceling
focus	focused	focusing

7. For nouns that end in "y", form the plural by dropping the "y" and adding "ies".

city	cities
fly	flies
penny	pennies

8. Learn the differences: they're/their/there; you're/your; we're/were; no one/none; all ready/already; though/through.

ARTICLES AND PREPOSITIONS

These are the most difficult rules to learn in English. Ask your teacher for the answer whenever in doubt, and study these rules.

ARTICLES

The articles in English are "the", "an" and "a". "An" and "a" are easy to use. They both refer to a singular, unspecified item. For example, "a cup of coffee" or "an apple". "A" is used with words beginning with consonants or vowels pronounced with consonants (e.g. the "u" in "used" /yuzd/, "a used car"). "An" is used before vowels or silent consonants followed by vowels (e.g. an honest woman).

"The" refers to a specific item. e.g. I want the book I lent you last week. It is not used with general items, as is so in many languages. For example, we do not say, "I like the sugar." We do say, "Pass me the sugar" if it's a specific bowl of sugar that we have in mind. This is true of plurals as well as singulars. For example, we do not say "The people are funny" if we are speaking about people in general.

PREPOSITIONS

Among the most common, yet problematic, prepositions in English are *at*, *in*, and *on*.
IN generally means "inside"; and "within" when referring to time.
AT generally indicates a location or a specific time.
ON generally indicates a surface, a specific day, or date.

Then there are hundreds of verb/preposition combinations, and these you simply have to learn one by one, e.g. think about, leave for, tire of, get married to, insist on, depend on, etc. Again, when in doubt, use a dictionary or ask the teacher for the correct preposition.

NEGATIVES

In English, we do not use double negatives. If we have a negative verb, for example, there may be no other negative words in the sentence. e.g. He didn't have any enemies. I didn't say anything. We didn't see anyone.
If we have a negated object, then the verb cannot be negative. For example: He had no enemies. I said nothing. We saw no one.

If we have a negative adverb, like "never", again, the verb must be positive. For example: I have never met her. {or) I haven't ever met her.

OTHER/OTHERS/ANOTHER

We use the word "other" as adjectives for plural nouns and "another" for adjectives for singular nouns.
e.g.   There are other ways of doing it./ There's another way of doing it.

We use the word "others" as the plural pronoun, and "another" as the singular pronoun.
e.g.   Some people didn't like him, but others said he was a good man.
         That was a great cup of coffee. May I have another?

REPORTED SPEECH

To report direct speech, put it in indicative word order, and move it back a tense. Also, change the pronouns as needed.
e.g.   He said, "I know her." - He said he knew her.
         I said, "We will do it." - I said we would do it.
         You said, "I haven't finished. - You said you hadn't finished.
To report commands, use "to" or "not to".
         He said, "Don't do it." - He said not to do it
         I told you, "Keep calm." - I told you to keep calm.

VOLITION

In English, if someone wants someone else to do something, but that thing hasn't yet been done, we generally use the infinitive. (Other languages use special verb forms for this special case, called the subjunctive.) We use the object pronouns as subjects of these clauses (me, you, him, her, us, them).

I *want John to mow* the lawn.
He *told me to go* jump in the lake.
I *urged him not to smoke*.
We *invited them to go* dancing.
She *commanded us to sit* down.
They *ordered us to leave*.
My teacher compelled me to study.
I *need you to be* there early.
He *forbid them to enter*.
I *warned them not to* speed.
He *implored us to lend* him the money.
My mother *sent me to do* the laundry.
They forced the child *to swallow* the medicine.
He advised me *not to sell* the car.

WISH and IF ONLY: special cases

After the verb "wish", we use the past for the present, and the past perfect for the past. For example:
I wish I *had* a lot of money. {a present wish) If only I *had* a lot of money.
He wishes he *had studied* harder last year. (a past wish)
If only he *had studied* harder last year.

PREFER, REQUEST, INSIST, DEMAND
These verbs are followed by "that", the person, and the base form.
I prefer/request/insist/demand *that he stay* inside.

CHAPTER ELEVEN

PREPARING YOUR BOOK

TYPING THE MANUSCRIPT

It is best, as I said before, if you write your book on a word processor. This makes revising extremely easy. Typing is the second most preferable form, because it is far more readable than handwriting. But it is very hard to revise typewritten pieces. The least preferable form is writing by hand, but if you must do this, remember: write on one side of the page only, use erasable pens, write on every other line of the paper, and have scissors and transparent tape available so that you may move or remove pieces of text.

ILLUSTRATING THE MANUSCRIPT

Some students like to illustrate their manuscript as they write; others prefer to do it at the end. Some have large drawings or pictures on separate pages in the text. Others prefer to put their illustrations on the left or right side of the page with the text on the other side. And some like to make spaces between lines of text and put their illustrations there.

There are various ways you may illustrate your text: with photographs, drawings, charts, maps, or computer graphics. You may take pictures from magazines, but you must acknowledge your sources. But readers usually like visual aids: they provide more information and a kind of intellectual relief as well. That is why magazines and newspapers use them, and many authors of books do so as well. Look back through this book to get some ideas for illustrating your own. If you are using a word processing program, probably that program has a graphics package that you may use.

TITLES

"Catchy" titles of books, stories, articles, and chapters of books entice readers to read on. Think about newspaper headlines, for example. They are brief, almost telegraphic, with few verbs, articles or inflections, yet they convey a good deal of information. Sometimes they are quotes or parts of quotes; other times they are just one word that says a lot. Go back over any pieces you have written so far. If you haven't titled them, do so. Then ask your group members for their opinions of your titles.

ORGANIZING YOUR BOOK OR MAGAZINE

Your book or magazine should have a cover, a hard one if possible. And on the cover should be the title of the book, in the center of the page and the center of the line, and in large letters. Then a little below it should be your name. Then your first page should also have the title, the author's name, the name of your class and school, and the year of publication.

On the next page you may dedicate the book to someone, giving his/her name, and perhaps a few words about why you are dedicating the book to that person. If necessary, you may write a foreword on the following page, if there is material you need to explain to the reader before s/he reads the book. The next page will be your table of contents, listing the chapters by number and name, and putting the page numbers of the chapter to the right. Then will come your text. Your text pages should be numbered at the bottom, beginning with Arabic number 1. Make sure to start each chapter on a separate page, number each chapter, and write the title of the chapter centered and in larger letters than the text itself.

Consult this book for examples. See how I wrote a title page, a table of contents with page numbers of chapter titles on it, and with a dedication. Also notice how each chapter begins on a new page and on the right hand side. Also notice the numbers at the bottom and center of each page.

SHARE AND CELEBRATE

During the last week of class, your teacher may set aside time for you to display the books you have written, and for the rest of the class to read them. I usually have refreshments and invite students and some of my colleagues to come in, have something to eat and drink, and sit down and enjoy reading one of the "books" on display.

SAVE YOUR "BOOK"

Be sure to save your book, because it will give you a lot of pride and satisfaction, and you may need it some day to show a future teacher what you can do as a writer. And **CONGRATULATIONS!**